MAROONED IN AGGIELAND

A BUMBLING BRIT DISCOVERS COLLEGE FOOTBALL, GUNS N' WAFFLES

BY JOSH PERRY

First published by Dog Ear Publishing
4010 W. 86th Street, Ste H
Indianapolis, IN 46268
www.dogearpublishing.net

ISBN: 978-1-4575-3215-3

Library of Congress Control Number: has been applied for

This book is printed on acid-free paper.

Printed in the United States of America

For Aggies across the world.
Oh, and Nigel, Michele and Alex.

TABLE OF CONTENTS:

INTRODUCTION:

Please note: I will not hold it against you if the contents of a burrito or pint of beer end up blemishing a portion of this book. In fact, I would be honored.

1. MENTALIST

"Third and nine. Let's see how many they bring. Again Mosley sneaks up. It looks like he's coming. He is. Manziel from the end zone, deep down the middle, he's got a man! Evans! Evans! Evans with a foot race! Michael Evans! They cannot stop him. TOUCHDOWN!"

Verne Lundquist, CBS announcer - 14.09.2013

With just over eight minutes to play in college football's most anticipated showdown of the 2013 season, I experienced the very reason why I gave up everything and chased something I vehemently believed in.

Texas A&M trailed Alabama by fourteen points, and found themselves in a precarious position on their own five-yard line. Kyle Field felt dormant. During a slog fest in the sweltering afternoon sun, it looked inevitable that the Crimson Tide would get revenge for November 2012's Battle of Tuscaloosa.

Out of nowhere, the Aggies cooked up a delectable moment that will stay with me for the rest of my days. Mike Evans' 95-yard touchdown sent every single person associated with the maroon and white into complete ecstasy.

Knowing I was there to witness such history made the $400 I paid for a ticket look like a glorious bargain. Eyebrows

3

might be raised at such a claim, because the Aggies still went on to lose 49-42. However, for me, that sporting memory will be one I will never forget. Why was it so significant? Because in those precious few seconds, I realized Texas A&M University had burrowed its way through my skin and into my blood.

After residing in College Station for several weeks, this place had blown me away. Never in a million years did I expect to become so attached to an American township and university. When I first arrived in Texas, I expected to feel like an embarrassed outsider looking in. In reality, I always felt at home.

I'm not afraid to admit that as Evans entered the south end zone, I wholeheartedly lost the plot. It was a pulsating, blissful and euphoric moment that sent me into sporting heaven. Most people have a handful of sporting memories they will never forget. This one went to the very top of my list. It's these moments that help us fathom why we put ourselves through the extreme ups and downs that sports can deliver. Back home in the aftermath of witnessing my beloved English soccer team, Portsmouth, lose almost every week, my mood reaches an all-time low. Friends and family that aren't enthusiastic about watching twenty-two athletes on a grassy mound kicking lumps out of each other, will ask me: "Why do you even bother?"

To be fair, it's a worthwhile question. I've repeatedly sat in a murky pub on a Saturday night, licked my wounds and thought: *What's the effin' point?*

A defeat will not only ruin the day, but the following week. The game will flashback at regular stages and turn sweet dreams into nightmares. That's not even taking into consideration the abuse dished out by contacts and co-workers that support one of the superpowers like Manchester United or Chelsea.

And yet, even after my team has suffered three relegations in four years, I keep going back for more, all in the veiled hope that as soon as our fortunes change, the bad times will help me to appreciate the good.

That's what the powerful and traumatizing world of sport can do to you. Once it's embedded in your veins, there is no going back. You're in it for the long haul, no matter how many sleepless nights it causes.

This isn't the case for everyone. These days you will almost certainly come across what I like to call the 'casual fan'. Definition: someone that doesn't idolize a world-renowned sport like soccer or football, but keeps up with it just so they don't look out of place when it's being discussed in a watering hole, such as a pub or bar. They will often pretend to support a trendy team to fit in with the crowd. Even though they claim to like an abundance of sports, they will secretly judge you for choosing to watch your team each Saturday in the bitter cold. They simply can't comprehend why you put yourself through it when you can relax in the confines of a distinguished armchair, sip tea, and passively gaze at the condensed highlights.

So, the minute I announced that I was going to give up my job, travel 5,000 miles and stay in Texas for numerous months, you can imagine the confusion and loud gasps that came from both the causal fans and non-sports lovers.

"Mate, you're a mentalist," cried one of the casuals.

I could sense people chatting behind my back, lambasting the whole idea. Even my girlfriend predicted I would only last a week before packing my bags and sprinting to the nearest airport.

It wasn't the fact I was leaving everything behind to go to an American state that's five times the size of England that shocked them. It was the reason. I was heading across the pond for one solitary factor: college football.

Deep down I felt like I was making the right decision. Following a stretch of selling my soul to the corporate world, I had reached the end of the line.

I was starting to feel robotic; my routine was slowly transforming me into a lifeless zombie. Each evening I'd get home from work, watch repeat episodes of mind-numbing sitcoms, and find myself getting out of breath as I devoured my body weight in sausage rolls and nachos.

Something had to give. There's only so many times you can wake up surrounded by empty packets of generic corn-based snacks, cheap cans of lager and half eaten microwave meals. In truth, I typified the lethargic world we now live in, a society where individuals feel the need to delve into forms of escapism and spend fifty hours a week immersing themselves into an unethical, suave character called Vince or Tony on a video game like *Grand Theft Auto*.

Eventually, the penny dropped.

It was late on a Sunday night. I was scrolling through online employment websites looking for one thing: hope. Unsurprisingly, I didn't have much luck. Working at Baguette Express did not appeal to me.

So, what was I going to do about it? How was I going to get out of this rut without having to join the eccentric world of sandwich making?

I sat and mulled it over. Literally minutes passed—nothing. I soon got hungry thinking of sandwiches.

And then it hit me. Whilst glancing at the television in the corner of my living room, ESPN Europe was broadcasting a compilation of grainy footage that showcased College Station's reaction to Johnny Manziel winning the Heisman Trophy.

From that moment, after several weeks of flirting with the idea, my mind was made up. Texas had emphatically placed itself on my horizon.

Although my inner circle heavily smirked at the concept of my adventure, it was time to grow some balls and do something drastic. When the email confirmation of my flights and living quarters came through, my future was set in stone.

From the day I announced my intentions to the day I left for the Brazos Valley, I was asked why I was going on this journey at least a hundred times.

My answers caused further bemusement. I couldn't really put it into audible words. Plus, none of my peers even understood what college football was.

I'm not going to lie; there were a handful of doubts that began to creep in. As my departure date grew closer and closer, the reality of what I was about to embark on loomed large.

Throughout this period, that age-old question remained. Why, why, why?

Hindsight is a wonderful thing, but as Mike Evans galloped the length of the field on that scorching day in mid-September, I finally had my answer.

That's why.

2. SWARMED

During the manic celebrations that followed Mike Evans' 95-yard touchdown, it's fair to say my actions ruffled the feathers of the people around me. Why? Because I was surrounded by Alabama fans in every direction. My seat was located just four rows behind their marching band in Section 149 of Kyle Field.

Granted, should I have spiked my water bottle into the sun-baked ground causing it to drench everyone? Probably not.

Regardless, I didn't care.

Up until that point, the folk from Alabama had been goading a reaction out of me; it was like a psychotic game of cat and mouse. To them, my maroon t-shirt was a sign of provocation. I was a slab of meat thrown to a pack of hungry coyotes.

When I received my ticket for the clash, I was warned I'd be amongst a generous grouping of 'bammers'. At the time, I had no idea what this phrase meant.

On the morning of the fixture, I decided to conduct a little market research into this supposed mob of Homo sapiens that I'd be sharing such a prestigious sporting juncture with. After a few searches online, I found myself browsing the infamous Urban Dictionary. Their definition of a bammer was:

A redneck, toolish, uneducated, obnoxious fan of the University of Alabama Crimson Tide football program. Most bammers have never set foot on the school's campus, much less taken a class or graduated from there, and don't care about any sport other than football. A bammer usually can't tell you anything about the University of Alabama unless it is football related. More intelligent bammers may know that the school is in Tuscaloosa, but don't count on it. Despite having absolutely no affiliation with the school besides liking their football team, bammers use the word "we" when talking about Bama football. They will also pick a fight over "their" school, especially if you talk smack about Bear Bryant. You are most likely to find bammers in trailer parks and in line to collect either unemployment or welfare.

Following this rigorous investigation, I safely presumed I'd be located next to some flavorsome Alabama football fans.

Half a dozen hours later, as I took my position in the stadium, I could already feel concerted eyes burning into the back of my head. Likewise, I heard comments such as, "Ha-ha. Look at this. We've got an Aggie to play with!"

Unfortunately for them, I wasn't in the mood to participate. That didn't stop gestures coming my way from various angles. I stood bewildered by the whole scenario. Back in England, stadiums use segregation between sets of supporters. The away fans are penned into the darkest, gloomiest corner. There would be no chance of a home fan accidentally finding his or her way into the opposition's pit like I had at Kyle Field. This is because there's absolutely no love between teams, only pure bubbling and vicious hatred.

Some home supporters actually get season tickets as close to the away section as possible, just so they can volley abuse at them for ninety minutes each week. They don't even watch the game. How sad is that? Coins are tossed, and on one occasion I saw someone get so flustered that he ripped a seat off its hinges and proceeded to chuck it in the direction of the opposition's fans.

I think the bammers suspected I would be easy prey. Little did they know, I had grown up on the terraces of one of Britain's most notorious and hardest football clubs.

The gameday experiences of English and college football could not be more different, which is fitting really, because the two sports are like chalk and cheese.

Going to an English football match is not for the faint-hearted. To kick the day off, a visit to the local 'greasy spoon' cafe is mandatory. This is an environment that serves one purpose: lining your stomach so you can consume as much alcohol as possible. The food will often be inedible, and in some cases may result in several days of abdominal pain, but you chomp it down regardless. Struggling to picture such an establishment? Visualize a Denny's that has been repeatedly burned down for insurance purposes. Now I've put that less than pleasant image in your mind, it's time to rectify it.

Imagine a beautiful, traditional pub. Plenty of genuine ales on tap, some cheerful pensioners sitting in the corner doing a crossword, cricket on the TV and a gentle landlady with a heart of gold behind the bar.

That's what a pub looks like six days a week. On a football matchday? Carnage.

The legal capacity will be oversubscribed tenfold, and it will genuinely look like an improvised explosive device has been detonated from behind a fruit machine. Broken glass, stained carpet and a combined smell of ale, cigarettes and urine will dominate proceedings.

Songs will be sung at volumes that burst your eardrums, and when I mean songs, people aren't singing about farmers fighting or urging their team to 'beat the hell outta' their opposition. Nope, these songs will involve every single unpleasant word under the sun. For example, if you're an away fan and you're scarily naive enough to breach a home-only pub, you will get a song such as, "You're going home in a f***ing ambulance" sung at you. Oh and then you'll probably end up in an ambulance, and spend the next three months walking with a severe limp.

English football fans with their fierce island mentality are weird and wonderful creatures. All week they will act as upstanding members of society (well, most of them anyway), but on a Saturday the gloves come off. It's the one day people let loose, drink as much as they physically can, enjoy some laughs and if someone looks at them funny, have a fight.

During fixtures, both sets of supporters will attempt to belittle each other via a variation of different songs and chants. I'll admit they are amusing, but if your child is in attendance you probably want to guarantee they are wearing some industrial-sized ear protectors.

My parents certainly wished they'd gone down such a route. I went to soccer every week from the age of six. A couple of weeks following my debut, we were watching a Premier League match on TV in our front room. Moments after the officials made a bad call, I immediately stood to my feet and belted out a song that suggested the referee liked to fondle himself in the privacy of his own home. To this day, I will never forget the look my mother gave me. Additionally, months later at my school's parents' evening, the teachers complained about my 'horrifically bad language' and stated that my newly acquired vocabulary had spread around the playground like wildfire. It was as if I was the dreaded child with head lice, but instead of distributing a horde of wingless ectoparasites, I was merely dishing out a selection of colorful phrases.

I received a telling off, but I didn't care. By that point it was already too late. I had been immersed into the culture of English football.

In the 1970s and 80s, circumstances were far worse— you'd get weekly death tolls. Since then, due to an upturn in policing, the stigma surrounding football hooliganism has cooled down. Conversely, there is still the odd occasion that makes you fear for your own safety.

From personal experience, the most recent case was when my club, Portsmouth, drew Southampton in the fourth round of the FA Cup in 2010. Quite frankly, these two cities despise each other. It's one of the deadliest rivalries in the United Kingdom. Every time they play there are multiple arrests, banning orders and the respective cities get ransacked.

The hatred dates back over a century. They have not only battled on the football pitch, but more significantly as merchant and naval ports.

Whilst the cup draw took place, I remember Southampton being pulled out of the hat first. I let out a gasp.

Next up, ball number 35. Portsmouth. Oh my word.

Ironically, I was living in Southampton at the time. As soon as the tie was announced, I knew there would be trouble. It had been five years since the two sides last met. That day in April 2005 was a bitter pill to swallow for Southampton fans—Portsmouth inflicted humiliation by romping to a 4-1 victory, which effectively relegated their nemesis to the league below. Now, there'd finally be a shot at revenge.

On the eve of the game, I was out in the city. You could sense the excitement, nerves and anticipation fluctuating in the air. Already the first of the 400 police officers expected at the event started to appear.

Following little sleep, I left my sheltered accommodation and walked into the direction of the stadium. On the way I meandered past a bridge that adorned a bed sheet covered in red paint hanging over the side. It read: "Portsmouth, WELCOME TO HELL."

That sentiment was a sign of things to come. As I approached the designated away section, I walked into some lively Southampton fans that were gesturing they were going to slit my throat. Classy. It wasn't anything I hadn't seen before, and it wasn't until after the ninety minutes that the volume was considerably ramped up.

Portsmouth had proven that lightning does strike twice. On this day they had won 4-1 again. This time though, it was in Southampton's own backyard. The locals were understandably irate and baying for blood.

During our jubilant exit of the ground, the police detected an air of unpredictability waiting for us around the corner. Barely twenty yards down the road, a disgruntled mob came charging towards us. They were throwing objects such as glass bottles, stones, flares and any other portable objects they could get their foul mitts on. It was nasty. Luckily, their aim was as poor as their team. The Bobbies chased them down a back alley, never to be seen again.

We were marched through the city back to the train station. There was a constant wall of police separating ballsy Southampton fans and us. This didn't stop the tribal hatred from boiling over, with many giving in to temptation and breaching the wall to engage in hand-to-hand combat.

At the halfway point I noticed one man and his adolescent son dismantling a bus stop. Each time they broke a piece off, they threw it in our direction. It was surreal. However, that wasn't the most unorthodox component. Throughout our stroll underneath an oncoming bridge, I noticed a light drizzle in the air, a warm spattering. In February? I was stumped. Then it hit me. A group of brainless corpses were urinating onto our heads. Lovely.

In the aftermath, dozens of people were rounded up and shoved into the back of police meat wagons. The trouble resulted in the legislation surrounding big rival derbies to be drastically altered.

Strictly speaking, English football fans do not take losing lightly. Another exchange that comes to mind was when I traveled on the official supporters' bus for a contest against Everton.

Whilst leaving the stadium, the vehicle slowly crawled through the city of Liverpool. Meanwhile, Evertonians streamed past us in their droves. Unsurprisingly, the abuse escalated. Before I knew it, the window to my left was smashed into a million pieces; several people had been cut by shards of disjointed glass and had blood pouring down their cheeks. A nutcase had dislodged a brick from one of the local houses and decided it would be a cracking idea to lob it at us. Also, some plucky goons attempted to hijack our wheels with Stanley knives before getting chased down the street.

These altercations do not solely occur in club football. On a national scale there have been some alarming cases over the years. One that immediately springs to mind was on the night that England got knocked out by Italy at the 2012 European Championships, some exasperated England fans thought it would be heroic to vandalize Italian restaurants, cars and clothes shops in local towns throughout the country. If that wasn't embarrassing enough, a couple of morons pelted a nearby Pizza Hut with rocks, completely ignoring the glaring fact that Pizza Hut is actually an *American* fast food chain. Sometimes there are no words to describe such idiocy.

Yes, I realize that I have labeled English football fans as wild, senseless Neanderthals. I fully expect when this book is released, James Bond or someone from MI5 to burst through my window and demand I appreciate my Queen and country more. In reality, do I consider the situation of our version of football bad? Not really. That's what I'm used to and what I've grown up on. I wouldn't change it for the world.

So, after witnessing a bevy of harrowing incidents, it would take a lot for the bammers to intimidate me. That didn't stop them, especially one bloke that was so tanked-up he barely possessed the ability to remain on his feet. Once he had shuffled along the row, I could immediately tell he'd be trouble. He pointed at the field and screamed at the top of his lungs, "MANZIEL! YOU SUCK, AND SO DOES YOUR MOM."

Clearly, with such highbrow insults at his disposal, this cheeky chappy was carrying around a fairly chunky thesaurus with him. As soon as he set eyes upon me, he proceeded to point the abuse closer to home. In one foul swoop, the Urban Dictionary definition had been justified.

Ironically, six weeks later, Fox College Football's sports journalist, Clay Travis, ranked Alabama's fan base as America's dumbest. I sympathized with his conclusion, especially when a bammer uploaded a picture on the internet of their new-born baby in an Alabama jumpsuit surrounded by a pink handgun, six rifles and a pistol.

On the flipside, they weren't all intolerable. Some sensed I was sticking out like a sore thumb and jokingly suggested I should wear some of their Alabama gear to hide my shame. I politely laughed and declined.

One aspect I failed to put my finger on was why the bammers insisted on waving hundreds of identical sticks in the air. These weren't any old sticks; they had miniature pom-poms attached. I quickly came to the assumption these inexplicable props had been created by the devil.

There was a group to my left that couldn't believe they'd been squeezed into the corner of the stadium. They were moaning that they might as well have been watching the game from the parking lot. Me? I wasn't bothered. I was merely happy to be there, although if you'd seen me at halftime you'd have probably thought differently.

After an electrifying inception for the Aggies, I was bloody loving it. Johnny Manziel and the offense had accumulated fourteen unanswered points. Suddenly, I was surrounded by a flock of tremendously mute bammers. With so long still to go, I didn't milk the situation as much as I could have. I was well aware that my actions had the capacity to come back and bite me on the backside. It ended up being a good call; Alabama led 28-14 at the midway point.

I went down in front of the Jumbotron to get a bottle of water; it felt like the Aggies needed a miracle to get back into contention. That's when something strange happened. As the

Crimson Tide players and coaching staff plodded out for the second half, I found myself standing directly adjacent to their dressing room door. Out of the corner of my eye, I noticed a diminutive man strolling out looking unbelievably pleased with himself—he looked like the cat that had got the cream.

It was their head coach, Nick Saban. The fourth highest paid sports coach in the whole of America. In a matter of moments he'd be two or three yards from me.

So many thoughts entered my sweaty head. On his approach, some Aggies nearby shouted some generic insults. He clearly heard and reacted by nonchalantly looking up at the scoreboard and smugly raising his eyebrows as if to say, "Remind me again, who's winning?"

This enraged them further. Unsurprisingly, more volatility was arrowed in his vicinity. That's when my potential moment flashed before my eyes.

Nick Saban was literally right in front of me and I had a full bottle of water grasped between my fingers. Should I soak him with it?

In one foul swoop, this footage could be all over every sports network within minutes. Plus, in a bizarre and unexplainable way, it might give the Aggies the catalyst they needed to somehow get back into the game.

What would happen to me if I did it? Would I be arrested? Or even worse, sent to Guantanamo Bay? Furthermore, what would my family think? Would they be proud of their hooligan son making a fool of himself just so he could rub the smile off a football coach they'd never heard of?

Eventually, the pending concept of being sent to Guantanamo Bay was the deciding factor. I'll be honest, I didn't fancy going there much, even though *Harold and Kumar* escaped with relative ease.

Do I have any regrets about not going through with it? Perhaps. Each time I see him on TV, I believe me and good ol' Nick have some unfinished business.

Astonishingly, it wasn't the fact that the Aggies were losing or because the bammers surrounded me like a shark that bothered me the most. Not even close; it was their marching band.

With such close proximity, I felt the full force of every time they played the same dreadful tune after a first down. And believe me, there were a hell of a lot of them that day— thirty-one to be precise. Imagine every few moments, for hours, being blasted with the repetition of a single ghastly tune. To top it off, following each rendition, I'd get thousands of people screeching, "Roll Tide!" into my ears.

Whilst this occurred, I couldn't take my eyes off of one of the marching band conductors, perhaps because at times it was easier to watch than AJ McCarron throwing his fourth touchdown pass of the day.

He was an unconventional chap that demanded complete perfection from his troops. Maybe he was Nick Saban's offspring?

After four and a half hours in the Texan sun, we were deep into the fourth quarter. The band's enthusiasm was understandably starting to relinquish, especially from the poor fellows that had cumbersome instruments slung over their bruised shoulders.

Anyway, this conductor wasn't in the mood to accept any forms of slacking. If any of the band members were a second late or out of tune, he'd deliver a deathly stare followed by a mouthful of expletives. It was remarkable, how was he getting away with it?

With this in mind, I unexpectedly found myself feeling sorry for the band that had caused such anguish up until that point. As I stood there enraged by his antics, I noticed a phone number appear on the Jumbotron that allowed members of the general public to report anti-social behavior.

It was time to take matters into my own hands. If no one was going to poleaxe the ladder he was standing on, it was down to me to slay the monster. Call me a tell-tale all you like, but desperate times call for desperate measures.

Before going through with it, I handed him a final shot at redemption. He threw it back in my face. Seconds later, he shouted at an overweight gentleman that was clearly dehydrated and struggling in the heat.

Like a flash, I delved into my pocket to recover my phone; I began to text the number on the big screen:

'Section 149: A good for nothing scoundrel is bullying a group of roughly 100 band members in front of me. He's standing on a ladder and is dressed like an idiot. Oh, and he's restricting my view of the cannon.'

Sent.

3. Don't Do Anything Silly

My last day at work was an eerie affair. In exactly one week, I would be in Texas.

That night after the obligatory ritual known as leaving drinks, I was on a midnight train to Georgia. Well, not exactly. I was actually heading to my humble abode in Guildford, Surrey. If you've never heard of Guildford, simply imagine an old, picturesque town that sits roughly 32.3 miles southwest of Central London and you'll be bang on the money.

During this train journey I pondered what the next few months might bring. Yes, this project had been planned for ages, but the reality of it always seemed so distant. Plus, in the meantime, normality resumed. I still went to work, still ate four and a half meals a day and more importantly, still had the odd beer or twelve.

Don't get me wrong; I was implausibly excited about my pending adventure. But as I left my job I couldn't help but notice record unemployment levels were being discussed on news bulletins every single day. Yet here I was, in full time employment and walking away from it. And for what? A town that I knew very little about? A state that doesn't pride itself on the quality of its fish and chips? A nation that has more time zones than the UK has skyscrapers?

That's not even taking into account the fact I was leaving for a sport that none of my friends or family could give a rat's arse about. Similarly, at this moment in time, thanks to an ongoing NCAA investigation, it looked a real possibility that a certain Heisman Trophy winner called Johnny Manziel might be banned for the entire season.

I'd put all my savings into these next few months, into my dream. It sounds harsh, but the thought of traveling thousands of miles to live in a one-star travel tavern, all to witness second-string quarterback Matt Joeckel throw a buffet of bubble screen passes, was rapidly losing its appeal.

I was taking the biggest gamble of my life. Was it too late to pull the plug?

Whilst mulling everything over on this train, something unexpected happened. Fifteen minutes in, we stopped at Crowthorne. I'd sat motionless at this station hundreds of times before. However, this time was different. I noticed a drained, rustic billboard hanging on a brick wall. From memory I can't recall what the image was, probably because I was so taken in by the words that stretched across the bottom. It read, "Fortune Favors The Brave."

Brave. It's a thought-provoking word. I'd usually associate it with people that fight for their country, battle cancer or take a stroll down an East London street after 8:00 p.m. Was I being brave? Or idiotic? Or both? Only time would tell. In seven days, I'd certainly have an inclination.

My remaining time in England frittered away. I got an early taste of what it felt like to be unemployed. Instead of doing important stuff like finding my passport or sorting out travel insurance, I sat on my couch, ate barely cooked pasta, and repeatedly punched my laptop as I tried to come to terms with another dodgy source claiming Mr. Manziel had illegally signed fifty billion pieces of memorabilia.

At one point it really wasn't looking good for Johnny. I didn't exactly consider this to be a good omen for my trip, especially with the lingering reminder that on the exact day I had booked my flights in mid-May, a spate of deadly tornadoes hit the Texas area, resulting in six fatalities.

I hadn't packed my bags yet and the whole enchilada was already going tits up. Things could only get better, right? Wrong. Two days before I was set to fly out, the motel I was due to stay in for the Alabama game weekend contacted me. They had overbooked; I was culled. Uh oh.

For the next few hours I frantically scrolled through the archives of the internet. I was naively praying that some place in the Brazos Valley would be able to accommodate a bumbling Englishman for a couple of nights. No matter how many variations of the words 'hotel, motel, accommodation, College Station, desperately urgent' I put into a search engine, nothing was available.

Each day seemed to bring a fresh kick in the groin. The thought of showing up at my old office on the following Monday and pretending that my resignation was all just a strange misunderstanding crossed my mind. Luckily, even for me, that would have been sinking to a new low. My self-respect and dignity would have been flushed down the proverbial toilet.

Regardless of these early hiccups, I wasn't going to give up. To soothe these growing pains, I did what any human being should do. Not comfort eating, but a phenomenon I like to call comfort watching.

Had a rough day? Is your boss giving you a hard time? Tired or bored? Well, there is a very simple cure. No, it's not pornography.

Re-watch Texas A&M's victory over Alabama from the 2012 season. It serves as the ultimate antidepressant. So, that's exactly what I did. It delivered a much needed reminder that I wasn't going on this excursion for a holiday or to worry about getting my first taste of homelessness in a couple of weeks.

Instead, I was going to complete what I originally set out to do. Go somewhere different to anywhere I'd ever been, enjoy the ride and hopefully stay alive to tell the tale. This trip was all about one thing: going to a unique place for a few months, fully discovering the behemoth that is college football and letting history take its course.

The beauty of the adventure was that I had absolutely no idea what to expect. For all I knew, I might hate the place and want to come home after 48 hours. How was I to know?

I certainly had a lot of time to deliberate. The night before I flew to Houston, I didn't sleep a wink. I was agitated. Was this whole idea as completely bonkers as I was starting to believe it was? Do people usually quit their jobs to fly around the world and experience university sports?

All these questions filled my overtired brain as I visited the toilet for yet another sit down wee in the dark. I couldn't take my eyes off the alarm clock. Every minute that went by was another closer to getting on that Boeing 747. I'd easily describe it as one of the most uncomfortable nights of my life. This, combined with all the sour omens leading up to my departure, and I was hardly filled with bundles of optimism.

Eventually it was time to depart my one-bedroom apartment and head to London Heathrow Airport. After bidding farewell to my girlfriend, who was rather pissed off that I was leaving for this merry jaunt, it was finally time.

My father, who lived abroad, was conveniently in the neighborhood and had come to pick me up. On the journey to Terminal 5, barely a word was spoken. There was no looking back—this was it.

As we said our goodbyes at the airport, he noticed I was traveling light for someone that wasn't exactly going on a quick vacation. He raised his eyebrows and left me standing on the sidewalk with the following words ringing in my ears, "Remember, don't do anything silly out there, son."

I unexpectedly laughed out loud. That whole sentence seemed rather ironic. After all, I was on the brink of doing something very silly indeed. I was scheduled to imminently trek across the planet to a random town in the middle of Texas for a sport that nobody I knew cared about and, to top things off, I'd soon be homeless.

Unsurprisingly, I hadn't told him about my precarious living situation. Little did he know, I'd spent the entire evening the day before looking at places in College Station that are open twenty-four hours a day. I had earmarked these locations to serve as somewhere I could stay out of trouble for the period I'd have nowhere to reside in. I'd even made a timetable so I wouldn't be in the same place for too long. I didn't exactly want to make it obvious that I was staying at these individual hideouts purely for their roofs.

The reason I was traveling light was simple. Before the Alabama weekend motel fiasco, I was all set to take a whopping big suitcase. Now, I was in no position to take one. How was I going to carry something so spacious when depressingly strolling the streets of the Lone Star State?

It reminded me of how farcical everything seemed. I was leaving my whole life behind, all in the name of college football and Texas A&M. Do you know what the most outrageous part of it all was?

Twenty-four months before, I didn't even like American football.

4. ADDICTED

"You're from England? And you're here to write about OUR football?"

Nine out of ten people would faint after asking the above. From day one, every person I met struggled to understand why I had hopped over the Atlantic to write about a sport that is not considered part of Great Britain's mainstream culture.

In one particular instance, an opinionated and mature gentleman called me a liar when I told him why I was in College Station—he simply couldn't get his head around my explanation and insisted I was playing a practical joke on him. I was not. He kept repeating the same two sentences: "Why did you travel all this way? Wouldn't it be easier to stay at home and cover soccer?"

Following an hour of trying to get my point across, he wasn't having any of it. Nevertheless, it didn't bother me. Fundamentally, I was ready for it. I knew I'd have to deal with similar comments for the next few months. In a way, it spurred me on more. It reinforced the notion that I was doing something unique. Plus, it was too late to back out; I was already engulfed in the heart of Texas.

His words about soccer resonated. Soccer was a black cloud that followed me throughout my entire stay in

Aggieland. People often asked me if I'd caught an Aggies soccer game. Of course it is a fair enough question, but I hadn't just swapped continents to get amongst a sport that I'm encircled by every minute of the day back home. Nope, I'd come to sample a culture that is downright alien to me.

The English and American sporting landscapes could not be more different. During my childhood, as a substitute for playing Little League Baseball or Pop Warner Football, I was brought up to appreciate crumpets, cups of tea, and the most significant person in the world: Queen Elizabeth II.

Well, that's not strictly true. I don't even like tea, but you can't beat a good old-fashioned stereotype. In terms of sports, England has three integral ones. Four if you include darts, which I don't.

The main one is football. This is universally known as soccer. To make it easier to digest, I'm going to stick with calling it soccer, even though my country may deport me for using such an unpopular Americanism. It's a well-known fact in British versions of the bible; it's listed as a sin to refer to our football as soccer. Please forgive me, Father.

When I was growing up, in the hours I wasn't buttering a scone or listening to stories of how my forefathers pranced around the world, I was doing one thing. Playing soccer. I was soccer crazy. Everything I did was somehow related to it. I'd never be located more than six feet from a ball or goalkeeper gloves. My hairstyle was based on my favorite player. One year I was given a birthday cake and it was not soccer-themed. It was the worst day of my life.

Throughout the early stages of my fascination, I reached a roadblock. On a regular Wednesday evening, a light bulb pinged in the depths of my limited intelligence. Once I had finished staring at my reflection in a pair of glossy shin guards,

I made a judgment call that in the mind of a six-year-old made perfect sense. From that day forward, young Joshua was no more. Instead, I wanted my friends, family and school teachers to address me by my newly desired name: Alan. For a solid week I tried my best to get this exotic alias to catch on. Why Alan? Because the soccer team I supported had four players that shared this heroic name. It was as simple as that.

Months before, I had witnessed my first Premier League game on TV. It was magnificent. Thousands of people were singing, jumping and dishing out abuse. This was a world away from being at the local park and kicking a tennis ball at a crippling wall. The Premier League was glitzy, glamorous and exciting. I was entranced by it.

Fast-forward a couple of decades and it's fair to say that I'm no longer fixated by soccer as I once was. I slowly became disillusioned with it. Instead of living and breathing the sport, I found myself preferring football of a different shape, style and country.

Why the transition? There are many reasons. In England, the league is not competitive. Between them, Manchester United, Chelsea and Arsenal have won the Premier League eighteen times in the past twenty years. People may enjoy watching the big guns battling it out, but there's only so many times you can watch the same ghastly, oil-rich teams frolicking with the desired silverware.

Compared to the NFL in the same period, there have been thirteen different winners of the Super Bowl. Likewise, you get the draft system that not only excites fans, it creates a level playing field. And there lies my predominant issue with soccer. Quite frankly, it isn't a level playing field. It revolves around one component—cold, hard cash.

Until a stringent spending or salary cap is introduced, it will be forever dominated by the powerful few. In the NFL, the Dallas Cowboys are worth the most at a gigantic sum of $2.3 billion. They haven't won a Super Bowl since 1995. That says it all. Well, perhaps it says more about the ownership of Jerry Jones, but that's an entirely different debate to be had.

So, how did I end up in this predicament? How did American football infiltrate my life? It's a story that dates back to my murky, anti-social teenage years. I had a friend called Nick McKenna who was besotted with American football. Each evening we'd stay up playing obscure computer games until unholy hours of the morning. He'd then sign off to watch Sunday or Monday night football. We had similar interests, so I thought I'd give it a whirl and watch a game with him.

Within five minutes I was mocking poor Nick. This sport seemed bizarre. I couldn't understand why the coaches were wearing headsets that were twice the size of their heads. The retro technology looked like it had come straight from the 1970s. Equally, I struggled to comprehend why there were so many commercial breaks. It felt like every couple of minutes I'd be subjected to a fresh round of blue chip companies trying to flog me another insurance plan or overpriced gadget.

Some aspects impressed me. It was clear that these games were always a huge spectacle. The big screens were the size of four-bedroom houses, stadiums were enormous, and fans were waving towels like their lives depended on it.

Shamefully, that was my first and last taste of the sport for a long while. In that period, Nick valiantly tried to get me more and more hooked with the NFL. He even suggested that I should support a team so I'd feel more of a connection to what was going on. Who would I support? I had no idea. Prior to this episode, my favorite times spent in the USA were embarrassingly at Disney World, Orlando.

For the next few weeks I was a diehard Miami Dolphins fan. The only problem was that during this wonderful period I kept referring to them as the "Florida Dolphins." Things hadn't got off to the best of starts. Nick believed I was a lost cause, and who could blame him?

He wasn't going to give up. A few years later, he got us tickets for New Orleans Saints vs. San Diego Chargers in an International Series game at Wembley, London. This was his last roll of the dice.

I remember approaching the stadium that day; I had no idea what to expect. When the first game came to London a year before, there were over 500,000 ticket applications. I found it irrational that so many people were into this form of football. In all my years, Nick was the only person I'd come across that had shown any indication they liked an American sport.

Yet here we were, in the capital of England, surrounded by jerseys of all the different teams. I'll admit, I didn't know many of the rules. In all honesty, all I really knew was that each team was trying to get the ball into the opposition's end zone, similar to rugby in how a team attempts to score a try.

I loved how you could drink alcohol in your seat whilst watching the game. That's a complete luxury in England. For soccer games, consuming beer in view of the pitch is illegal.

Unfortunately, downing frequent beers didn't exactly help me in my bid to understand what was happening on the field. The game passed me by. As we exited the stadium, my awareness of the afternoon stretched as far as knowing New Orleans had been victorious and that there was something nicknamed a Hail Mary at the end. Who was Mary? Was she a regular feature?

I went away from that experience with a newfound respect for the sport and pledged I'd try to stick with it.

Such a vow lasted two weeks. Throughout that fortnight I still hadn't come to grips with the rules, and the games I watched simply didn't live up to the excitement and hype of Wembley. And sadly, there were no more sightings of mysterious Mary.

Several years later, I was in my early twenties, still living with my parents and had graduated from university. One day I was sitting in my bedroom after a long day at work when I was called down for a chat. Now everyone knows if one of your parents summons you downstairs for anything other than breakfast, lunch or dinner, something bad is probably going to happen.

The minute I entered the kitchen, I sensed an unusual atmosphere lingering in the room. My mother was cowering in the corner whilst my dad hovered over the kitchen table. *Bloody hell. What's going on here?*

"Josh, you may want to sit down. Your dad has some news," my mum declared.

Before I had time to react, the following words struck me like an axe: "Yes, I've got a new job … in Pittsburgh. Me and your mother will be moving there in six weeks."

Splat. I did not that see that coming. I had braced myself for an adverse notification, but my family moving away? Obviously, I wasn't a kid anymore, but my only sibling already lived in Washington DC. I was now going to be the only Perry left in Europe—the last man standing. I was the youngest in my family and didn't know what to think.

Ten minutes earlier I was happily going about my business, feet up and looking forward to watching an array of trashy evening television. Then bam! In one foul swoop, everything changed. Don't get me wrong; my folks weren't hanging me out to dry. They vowed to make the transition as smooth as possible. Plus, they said I could regularly visit them. Needless to say, I planned to milk such an invitation.

One week later, the three of us traveled to Pennsylvania for a couple of days to allow them to gain an early grasp of their new neighborhood. Whilst approaching the Steel City in the plane, the first thing I noticed was Heinz Field sat on the riverside. The golden seats stood out like shining treasures on the skyline. Heinz Field is the spiritual home of the Pittsburgh Steelers. My knowledge of the Steelers was minimal at best. All I knew was they had a quarterback that shared a nickname with London's most famous tourist attraction: Big Ben.

After departing the airport, we were taken up Mount Washington. It has a breathtaking view of the city. And there she was, Heinz Field, up close and personal. Simply looking at the stadium was captivating. I admired how the football and baseball stadiums were situated slap bang in the middle of the city. In many ways, it represents that the heartbeat of Pittsburgh revolves around its traditional sports.

When you walk around the perimeters of the district, every single person wears an item of clothing that proudly brandishes the Steelers logo. I'd never seen anything like it. I'd been to New York, Washington DC, Florida and Los Angeles, and had never come across a population that seemed so fanatical and partisan. I'll admit it was a little infectious. It made me crave a Steelers' jersey, mug, mouse mat … you name it; I wanted it just to fit in with the crowd!

The only problem was, I still hadn't grasped a basic understanding of the sport. My lack of knowledge surrounding the rules plagued me. There was no use looking the part in a Ben Roethlisberger or Troy Polamalu jersey if I had no idea what was going on during the games.

That trip came and went in the blink of an eye. It made me rather envious that I wasn't joining my parents on their Pittsburgh adventure, but I had found a suitable distraction in the form of football.

In those few days, the sport had somehow pinched my interest like never before. I vividly remember going to work the next week and being as productive as a deceased goat. Why? Because I spent the whole time studying the NFL, its history and more importantly, those damn rules. I was addicted. Every minute of the day I would either be reading a book, listening to a podcast or watching a documentary about football. It was like I was cramming for an exam, only there was no exam. It was a new pastime that I genuinely couldn't get enough of.

Some people drink alcohol, take drugs, gamble or sleep with as many people as they can. Me? I was only interested in one thing. My new obsession. I wanted to inhale football non-stop. There was so much to learn, from how the sport was born to the status of the modern game. Simply speaking, I had mountains of knowledge to absorb. In the English Premier League there are twenty clubs that list a squad of eighteen players every week. Compared to the NFL, this was a cakewalk to digest. I almost fainted as soon as I found out each of the NFL's thirty-two teams have a roster of fifty-three players. Moreover, these athletes aren't solely placed on the offensive or defensive side of the ball. There was something phantom called Special Teams to read up on, too. What was so special about them? What did they do?

Each day would bring bundles of exciting information. I had even reached the point where I'd ask my girlfriend, Katie, to test me on naming all of the franchises. Finally, I was beginning to differentiate between a Buffalo Bill and a St. Louis Ram. Although awkwardly, it did take me a couple of months to realize that Jim and John Harbaugh are, in fact, two different people.

If there was such an entity as rehab for football addiction, I needed to be admitted. This certainly became apparent when during a conversation with my co-workers about the differences between soccer and American football, I found myself angrily laying into my nation's pride and joy. They looked at me like I'd slapped them in the face with a wet smelly fish. They were wondering what on earth had happened to me. Had I been brainwashed in Pittsburgh? All signs pointed to yes. At one stage I even considered that maybe I had been. The turnaround could not have been more radical.

Funnily enough, they didn't raise the topic of soccer in front of me for a good few weeks after that. I was quickly alienating myself. I now appreciated how my old pal Nick McKenna felt all those years ago. He wanted someone to share his seemingly extraterrestrial passion with. Now I was in the same boat.

Suddenly, Sundays had turned into my new favorite day of the week. NFL Day. In the UK, our cable provider, Sky Sports, broadcasts what they perceive to be the most attractive early and late afternoon games. Therefore, I'd be sitting there for seven hours taking it all in. This came with a series of noticeable complications. I wasn't only unsettling my co-workers with this new hobby of mine; Katie wasn't exactly impressed with it either. Out of nowhere soap operas, romantic comedies and documentaries about polar bears were off the menu in favor of a sport she, like everyone else I knew, refused to give the time of day.

It didn't end there. Oh no. Throughout this period we had booked a romantic weekend away to Barcelona. Naturally, this meant I had to take it on the chin and miss an NFL Sunday. Or did I? Just the thought of it turned my stomach. Furthermore, the Steelers were playing the Baltimore Ravens in a highly charged AFC North showdown. I plainly could not miss it. Unbeknown to Katie, I spent the week leading up to our getaway looking for one thing: a bar that showed football. Following hours of trawling through websites, maps and reviews, I found a promising venue.

Once we got to Barcelona, it was time to put my mischievous plan into action. Leading up to Sunday, I'd been on my best behavior. Anywhere she wanted to go, I went with a smile. This included walking eight miles. Usually this would bring about one of my finest qualities: moaning. Did I say anything? Not a chance. I kept my nut down and served my time; I had my eyes firmly on the prize.

Eventually, Sunday night rolled around—it was time to dance with the devil. We were back at the hotel when the conversation about what to do later popped up. I played it cool. Rule one: Never show your hand too early. As the discussion progressed, I dropped some subtle hints about how I wouldn't mind going for a few drinks, and that I'd seen a sophisticated bar on our eight-mile trek the day before.

In reality, had we walked past this bar? Not even close. It was the venue I had up my sleeve all weekend. She agreed that after dinner we'd go and check it out. Result.

The only hindrance was getting dinner out of the way. As it was our final evening, we fancied visiting a location that served inconceivably high-priced grub. And when I say that, I mean somewhere that didn't just serve pizza, steaks and burgers. The first place we attempted to gain entry to quoted us a wait of one hour. Normally I wouldn't turn my nose up at such a delay. If anything, that time can be spent enjoying a bottled beer at the bar, no big deal. However, tonight was different. A dead hour had the capacity to cause havoc with my master plan. The timings would be out of sync; I had to think on my feet.

Ultimately, we decided to move on and try somewhere else. On our approach to the next posh eatery, I was repeating the same request in my head: *Please don't be busy. Please don't be busy.*

As we entered and went through the pleasantries of requesting a table for two, those beautifully soothing words came out of the waiter's mouth, "Come right this way." We were in. The dream of catching some NFL was alive and kicking.

An hour later, I was longing to pay the bill. The waiter was nowhere to be seen. I sat there restless. In my mind I was picturing the first downs, touchdowns and interceptions that I was missing. It wasn't a pleasant feeling.

Once I had frantically waved in the direction of an alternative waiter, we were granted the ability to reimburse the restaurant for their satisfying spaghetti carbonara, risotto and breadsticks. Needless to say, we left the establishment in a speedy manner. The next hurdle was to try and find the bar that was potentially showing football. Some reviews mentioned that it only showed the big games. In my albeit crammed knowledge of the sport to that point, I considered the Steelers-Ravens matchup to be one of the more reputable ones. As we came within reach of the place, out of the blue I realized that "big games" might just refer to the playoffs and Super Bowl.

I started to panic. The fact it might not be showing the game wasn't my only obstacle. From the outside, this bar looked like a filthy monstrosity. I hadn't even considered what it might look like or whether we may get stabbed while drinking there.

After looking at Katie's face, no words needed to be muttered. If this was my idea of having some romantic drinks on our last night, I sure wasn't going to be getting lucky afterwards.

Things only got worse. Well, for her. As we took a deep breath and entered, colossal TV screens and projectors surrounded us. What were they showing? A plethora of NFL coverage. I'd entered heaven. Katie had entered hell.

Mission accomplished.

It makes me chuckle when I look back at those wintery days. I was completely oblivious as to how much football had overtaken my life. Was I using it as a distraction to get away from the realization that my family had moved to the other side of the world? Had I fallen in love with something American just so it would make me feel closer to them? Or was it simply a bloody good sport I'd never given proper attention to?

Whatever it was, I was grateful. It filled a hole. Whilst my disillusionment with soccer became stronger, my adulation for football took its place.

Before my parents relocated, for almost two decades I'd spent every Saturday going to watch Portsmouth with my hero: my dad. It was always the one day of the week we'd spend together. Growing up, those trips to Fratton Park or to away games up and down the country will always remain at the forefront of my most cherished memories.

Each Saturday followed a similar path. I'd wake up basking in the knowledge it was the weekend, and be optimistic that our team might win later that day. We'd then set off on our mission to the south coast. On our journey we listened to sports radio and munched on the packed lunches that my mother had prepared for us. In all those years we always had the same meal. Ham and cucumber sandwiches, crisps, and a portion of mini-cocktail sausages. Utter bliss.

Once he moved to Pittsburgh, it marked an end of an era. I still had my season ticket and went to games but in the words of Johnny Manziel's chum, Drake—nothing was the same. Something was missing. I didn't enjoy it. Don't get me wrong, I will always support my team until the bitter end, but when your routine has been the same since you were three feet tall and it drastically changes, your heart isn't quite in it anymore.

I'm not afraid to admit that I went through some dark times. I was still living in the family home. The day they moved away was extremely difficult. For the first time, I came home from work and no one was there. Usually, as soon as I'd open the front door, our three cocker spaniels rushed to greet me. Now it was like a ghostly household after a zombie invasion. Thankfully, it was minus the dead bodies—and the zombies.

Several months later, the most tragic day was yet to come. I look back on it now with equal laughter and regret. It was Thanksgiving. In the weeks leading up to this turkey-filled holiday, I noticed Americans celebrate the occasion by having three back-to-back NFL games. Genius. I immediately ran to the nearest floor manager and booked the day off work.

Unfortunately, I'd made a rookie mistake. Because of the obvious time difference, the first game didn't actually start until 17:00 GMT. I could have easily gone to work and only missed the first half of the opening game. Despite this, I wasn't going to let my error dampen my spirits. If anything, it gave me ample time to prepare what I named that day: "El Feasto." It was exactly what it says on the tin: a sizable Thanksgiving banquet.

Here comes the tragic part. The meal was for one. Later that evening I spoke to my parents and brother via Skype, and saw them in a Christmas day-esque setting, jolly from the festivities and even more jolly from all the wine they'd consumed.

Yet there I was, in our old, empty and soulless family home, on my own, eating and drinking the pain away. It was like something out of a pathetic romantic comedy. As I swigged on cheap lager and took another bite out of a plastic, tasteless roast potato, I felt like a joke.

The third Thanksgiving clash didn't finish until nearly 4:00 a.m. Off the back of one hour of sleep, I was up for work. I was exhausted and disgustingly hungover.

That morning I was waiting in the freezing cold at the train station. Instead of being positioned at my usual spot on the platform, I was on my knees with my face down vomiting into the dark, shadowy and foul underbelly of a public toilet. Rock bottom.

Every day I looked up into the black icy skies and stared at the planes that accompanied the flight paths overhead. I'd often stand motionless, dreaming about being a passenger on one and heading out of my languid, unfulfilling routine that had reached the pitiful depths of no longer eating meals with a knife because it saved adding another instrument to the towering washing-up pile.

When I arrived at work, I reflected on the bigger picture. Whilst entrenched in thought, someone who worked on a team next to mine was enjoying his final day with the company. I'd never spoken to him but couldn't help overhear him chatting to some people nearby. He was leaving in order to chase his dream of becoming an artist. He claimed that if he stayed at the office any longer, he'd end up staying for the rest of his life. It was a cliché, but it hit me hard.

What was I doing? I hadn't even thought about what I wanted to do with my life. He had it all mapped out. I was in awe. All I could dwell on was my distinct unhappiness. I was sick of feeling like a joke. I couldn't even book a day off work without making a dog's dinner of it.

It was time to stop moping around and do something about it. It was time to chase my dream. My only problem was at that point I didn't know what my dream was.

However, I would soon find out.

5. BEHEMOTH

I will be brutally honest and admit that during my NFL addiction, college football sat quietly in the background. Whenever I came across it, the whole concept seemed outlandish. The sheer enormity of it threw me off balance. Why? Because in England there is nothing remotely like it.

The NFL and Premier League can draw startling comparisons because they are both corporate machines that are shaped to create the most marketable brand possible.

College football is different. It's more traditional, authentic and original. I didn't realize this overnight. It was an evolving process that not only changed my perception of the sport, but the culture surrounding it.

I wanted to prove I wasn't alone in finding the idea of college football hard to comprehend. Subsequently, I undertook an embarrassingly small case study. How? By confronting the streets of my hometown and asking random people about their opinions on college football.

Things didn't start well. Around my way if you approach a stranger on the street and you're not immediately told to 'f*** off', it's a bonus. Within minutes I'd been given countless cold shoulders. After the seventeenth person had told me to mind my own business, I decided to heed their advice.

Feeling despondent, I felt like cheering myself up by visiting the one place in the world that truly understands me—the pub. As the beers flowed, I had an epiphany. Where better to conduct my research than in a place full of chirpy and merry folk? I took a moment to pat myself on the back for such ingenuity.

Before I knew it, I was deep in conversation with five chaps that were stunned by the haphazardness of my enquiries. Regardless, they had a lot to say:

> "College football? Don't they get something silly like 100,000 people turning up at games?"

> "I heard they prefer college teams over their professional teams. Imagine preferring the University of Surrey over Chelsea? Madness."

> "I remember reading about some player called Tim Tebow. He's seen as the second coming of Christ. They are nuts out there."

> "Don't they have annoying marching bands that play throughout the game?"

> "I once saw some footage on Youtube of an eagle flying into a college stadium because it was their mascot. I just don't get it."

Those are a few snippets of the general conversation. Others I later asked chipped in with similar musings. It was clear there were a number of recurring themes. It was eye opening, because I related to them all. I mirrored these exact sentiments when I first came across college football.

Years before liking the sport, I could remember lazily flicking through an amalgamation of TV channels in a New York hotel. Nine out of ten were showing something labeled "Bowl Season." I hadn't a clue what this meant, but I was as equally impressed as I was confused.

Sitting on the edge of the hotel bed, I observed stadiums that were packed to the rafters. I didn't have to see much else. That single notion bamboozled my senses. To me, it was essentially a bunch of 19 and 20-year-old kids playing for their school. What's exciting about that?

In the UK, only two university sporting events are lucky enough to attract national coverage. These are the Varsity Match (rugby) and Boat Race (rowing) that take place annually between Oxford and Cambridge. Realistically, no one actually cares about the outcome. In essence, it's primarily an excuse for a bunch of toffs and posh people to bathe in their own self-importance.

When you compare the pageantry and passion of college football to my university and our soccer team, it's scandalous. University stadiums do not exist. You won't find anything like Kyle Field, The Coliseum or Beaver Stadium, on any English campus. Instead, you will find a wet, marshy field with less than convenient parking in the middle of nowhere. Likewise, in terms of fans or alumni turning up, think again. Even for big games and cup finals, you'd do well to find six people and a dog in attendance.

Different worlds. Yet across the pond, numerous college stadiums are bigger than those in the NFL. The thought of an English university having a stadium bigger than Manchester United is comical. And yet in places like SEC country, it is reality. These high-profile college players are on sports channels every minute of the day. They are mammoth celebrities before they've even graduated. Soccer players don't attend university, so that culture is non-existent in Europe.

Such a first impression put college football onto my radar. Even though I wasn't engrossed with the sport or really knew what was going on, I was intrigued. Little did I know, eight years later I'd up sticks in order to gain a further glimpse of the behemoth.

Naturally, when you like something, you find yourself wanting more of it. After falling head over heels for the NFL, it was time to push the boundaries. At this stage of my football addiction, I was willing to give anything a try—even the Canadian Football League.

During the offseason leading up to the 2012 campaign, I was struggling with the cold turkey process. Football was scarce and I badly needed a fix.

People claim you should never wish your life away. Even these people would have understood my predicament. Turning to the CFL for solace was a particular low point. The wait for the NFL season had broken me.

There I was on yet another dull and gloomy football-free weekend when some blurry CFL highlights popped up on TV. It wasn't particularly pretty or enthralling, but it was football. Well, sort of. To be honest, I'd been starved of the sport for so long it could have been three heavily stoned blokes in the street lobbing a pigskin around and I would've been just as hooked.

Instead, the NFL's neglected Canadian relative won a viewer. Consequently, I now had the confidence to go into a bar and discuss the quarterback situation of the Saskatchewan Roughriders. Get in line, ladies.

Needless to say, my infatuation with the CFL didn't last long. As much as I convinced myself I enjoyed that the Canadian commentators sounded like Julian and Ricky from the TV show *Trailer Park Boys*, it ended up serving as a short-term solution that was put to bed as soon as NFL training camps commenced.

During this time, the lead up to the college football season was heating up. I listened to dozens of discussions comparing both formats. A lot of people were adamant that college football was better than the NFL. I struggled to accept this, but who was I to argue with them? I hadn't given college football a fair chance to win me over. However, this soon changed.

With the college season only weeks away, I planned to throw myself into the deep end. Throughout lunch breaks at work, I watched a documentary series called "Rites of Autumn - The Story of College Football." It helped me to appreciate the history, rivalries and deep roots of the collegiate level.

Unfortunately, it couldn't explain everything. There seemed to be so many different divisions and schools—hundreds of them. Where was I even meant to start?

College Football for Dummies suddenly found its way into my online shopping basket. Before confirming the order, I pulled out. How hard could it be? The college system seemed baffling. I had absolutely no idea how it all worked, but I refused to waste £15 on a book that had the potential to muddy the waters even more.

Reading the explanation on Wikipedia was about as helpful as reading a Chinese food menu without English translation. Even after digesting it seven times, I still couldn't make sense of it.

Compared to the NFL, it seemed like you needed a degree in rocket science to understand it all. Aspects like the coaches' poll and the fact some phantom computer works out who makes it to the National Championship game almost pushed me over the edge.

I wasn't about to throw in the towel. As strange as it sounds, the more it puzzled me the more it intrigued me. One way or another, I was determined to get to grips with it. Furthermore, with the season about to get underway, members of the media were acting like Christmas was coming early. There seemed to be a unique anticipation surrounding the imminent campaign. Maybe it was because we'd gone so many months without football, or possibly because college football is statistically America's third favorite sport behind the NFL and baseball?

Overall, I didn't care. My mind was made up. I was going to watch as much college football over the next few days as I humanly could.

At the beginning of September 2012, I finally got my first proper taste of NCAA Football.

I was at the mercy of ESPN Europe. To be honest, I don't remember the exact games they showed that weekend, but I do vaguely remember sitting through Michigan at Alabama. Each showdown brought an invigorating spectacle to my screen. Compared to the NFL, college football immediately felt more stripped back. The passion and atmosphere was palpable.

On the other hand, I wasn't completely won over. Most of the matchups I observed were blowouts. The actual football and narratives on show didn't seem to be as alluring as the NFL. That left me feeling disappointed. As great as the stadiums and pageantry were, watching teams get pasted by 50 points felt a little underwhelming.

In the aftermath, I had mixed feelings. My first impressions of college football had been indifferent. There were plus points, but I didn't fancy watching teams get repeatedly destroyed each week. It reminded me of the NFL age-old saying: *The league is only as good as its weakest team.* Yet that Saturday I saw one college outfit who looked like they'd barely played the sport before.

Luckily for me, I rolled the dice again. With the NFL starting the following weekend, I decided to treat myself to a football marathon. With this in mind, I wanted to do things a little differently. I came to the conclusion that if I supported a particular university, I'd become more engrossed into what was going on.

The problem was, who the hell would I support? Obviously, I hadn't attended any of these universities and to be honest, I could only name a handful of them. Some options immediately sprung to mind, one being the University of Southern California. This was the first university I had ever heard of. My old mate Nick McKenna's favorite player was Reggie Bush. As a result, he had his jersey from his USC days. Moreover, the Steelers' stalwart, Troy Polamalu, was also a Trojan.

The other frontrunners were Pittsburgh and Penn State. With my parents living in close proximity to both, they seemed like a no brainer. I'd be able to watch either with relative ease.

After researching all three, I was back to square one. USC is based on the West Coast, so all of their games are shown at the dead of night in the UK. Pittsburgh played at Heinz Field, which at first I considered a plus point. On the other hand, once I'd watched some videos I soon noticed they barely filled half of the stadium.

That left Penn State. This seemed the most logical and attractive option. In spite of this, there was a large, dark and opaque cloud hanging over PSU. I'd discovered they'd been embroiled in an extremely serious child sex abuse scandal. News broke in 2011 that their assistant coach, Jerry Sandusky, had sexually assaulted at least eight underage boys. Officials at the university elaborately tried to cover up the incidents. However, everything eventually became public knowledge and Sandusky was sentenced to a minimum of 30 years in prison.

My idea of choosing a team was put on the back burner. With the NFL soon getting underway, I was happy just watching this next round of college games and hoping for a decent game that wasn't a 49-3 annihilation.

Then again, this time felt slightly different. I was getting my first taste of ESPN's College GameDay. It was being transmitted from College Station, Texas. They were there for Texas A&M's first ever game in the Southeastern Conference. Their opponents? The Florida Gators.

The pundits on the GameDay panel predicted this Texan outfit would do well to win a couple of games in 2012. I sat there thinking, *Oh great, I can't be arsed to sit through another blowout.* There and then, I intended to only watch the first quarter or two.

In spite of my misgivings, after interviews were broadcasted with the respective head coaches, I found myself warming towards Kevin Sumlin—A&M's man at the helm. He was an imposing and charismatic figure that spoke with genuine passion about his university and football program. I was spellbound with every word. This guy personified class and confidence.

Meanwhile, as the panel continued to lambast A&M's chances, I couldn't take my eyes off the structure that lay dormant in the background. It looked like something from Eastern Europe. A huge concrete construction that was so towering, it probably overlooked Mexico.

Out of nowhere ESPN showed some footage of Aggie traditions, such as midnight yell practice.

My jaw hit the floor.

The ESPN feature informed me that 30,000 people had got together on the previous evening to conduct a tribal sing-song. What threw me the most was they portrayed it like it was an everyday occurrence that was in no way abnormal.

I sat there frantically Googling it. Within minutes I'd watched six or seven midnight yell clips. ESPN wasn't pulling my leg. This was real. The weekend before I hadn't seen anything like this. Don't get me wrong, some aspects were impressive, but nothing jumped out of my TV screen and slapped me in the face quite like this place called Texas A&M had.

Funnily enough, midnight yell was barely the tip of the iceberg. Everything about this university seemed unique. It was like no place I'd ever seen before. My brain was sizzling. As I sat starry-eyed watching events unfold, my thirst for more knowledge grew larger. Ultimately, I had to put my laptop down. The game was about to kickoff.

Completely out of the abyss, I began to passionately support this team. I stopped to consider why I was rooting for them with such vigor—it was an unanswerable question. There was purely something about this place. The stadium, fans and atmosphere all rolled into one as it hit me from the other side of the Atlantic Ocean.

The previous week, I hadn't felt a connection to any of the countless universities I'd watched. When it comes to sports teams, you often choose who you want to support or, as in my case, your father chooses for you. This was different. I felt connected to Texas A&M. It was as if they had somehow chosen me.

Yes, I'm fully aware of how irrational that sounds. But I had no link to Texas A&M before that evening. I'd never been anywhere near the State of Texas or even knew what the "A&M" stood for. Yet here I was, willing them to win like my life depended on it.

That game wasn't just special to me because it was my first taste of Aggie football. It was significant because it was the coming out party of a 19-year-old kid called Johnny Manziel. Watching him perform was genuinely entrancing; it was like poetry in motion.

At halftime, A&M was leading 17-10. The dream was alive. Oh, how I wanted the ESPN experts to look boneheaded following their earlier predictions. Unfortunately, it wasn't to be. The Aggies failed to score a single point in the second half and ended up losing 20-17.

I was sad and confused. Why was I downbeat? A few hours before I had never even heard of Texas A&M. Yet here I was, mourning a loss.

It was a bug that stuck with me. Throughout my next week at work, I covertly read up on the background of this curious place that I had learned was affectionately known as Aggieland. Moreover, I discovered "A&M" stood for "Agricultural and Mechanical."

It was a whirlwind of events. One minute, I sat there wondering if I could even be bothered to watch another college football game; the next I was fixated with a university football team that hadn't won a National Championship since 1939.

Looking back, I still don't quite know how it all happened. How was I drawn to this place so much? At the back of my mind, I knew I had to go there. I needed to experience Aggieland for myself.

6. The Hunger Games Meets Survivor

A
s well as discovering Texas A&M on that fateful evening, my initial concerns surrounding college football had been put to bed. Finally, I had witnessed an exciting game that rivaled anything I'd seen in the NFL.

From that day onwards, I made a conscious effort to watch the remainder of Texas A&M's 2012 schedule. In truth, I was spoiled rotten. The Aggies romped to an 11-2 record, a victory in the Cotton Bowl, and quarterback Johnny Manziel became the first ever freshman student to win the much-coveted Heisman Trophy.

Even as I enjoyed victories in the SEC over teams such as Ole Miss and Arkansas, the thought never realistically crossed my mind that I'd ever go to Texas and live through the wonders of Kyle Field in person. Yes, as I sat there throughout the Florida season-opener, part of me longed to get a taste of what college football is like, but in all honesty, it always seemed an unrealistic pipe dream.

The first time I even contemplated flying to Texas was during A&M's crazy matchup against Louisiana Tech at Independence Stadium. It was one of the most ludicrous games of sport I'd ever seen. The final score of 59-57 looked more at home on a basketball court. Once it ended, I sat in silence for a good few minutes. I could barely get over what I'd just observed—it was the epitome of a shootout. That game promptly made me realize I'd fallen for college football in the same way that I had for the NFL.

Despite feeling a strong connection to this university in Texas, at that point, did I consider myself as an Aggie? Of course not. I loved watching them play, but I don't think you can truly become attached to somewhere if all of your experiences are rooted from a sofa on the other side of the planet.

Even so, something about this team charmed the pants off me. Compared to all of the other colleges I'd watched, none grabbed my attention quite like the Aggies. Every week, I'd be drawn to watching Coach Sumlin's troops.

Four weeks after the bonkers Louisiana Tech game, A&M traveled to Tuscaloosa to play the ultimate college football superpower, Alabama. The Aggies caused the upset of the year by slaying the Crimson Tide in their own backyard, 29-24.

At that stage I'd shown emotion towards Texas A&M, but this was on another level. As Deshazor Everett came down with the match-winning interception, jubilation consumed me.

With an extra step in my stride, my idea of traveling out for a game became more prominent. I looked at the upcoming schedule and saw there were two consecutive home games before the regular season came to a close.

Once I'd looked at flights for the curtain call against Missouri, my hopes were dashed. As I was looking so late, the prices were sensationally magnified.

Deflated, I came to terms with the notion I'd miss out on seeing heroic Aggies like Ryan Swope, Luke Joeckel, Damontre Moore, Spencer Nealy and Sean Porter in the flesh.

Not all was lost. Star players such as Johnny Manziel, Mike Evans and Jake Matthews were returning for the 2013 season. This meant if I wanted to see them play in maroon before they swanned off to the promised land of the NFL, I'd have to pencil in a trip for the following year.

My decision had been made—in twelve months I'd make the trip to Aggieland, one way or another.

Soon enough, the college football season was over. All the plans I'd cooked up were briskly put to one side. Real life took over and propelled me back into the routine of scrolling Netflix for under-rated documentaries about sharks and a diet of Cheetos and fizzy cola.

A couple of months later, I had the most vivid and disturbing dream of my existence. The events and emotions felt so lifelike in a sleepy, concoction of feelings that were reminiscent of a nightmare.

When I gained consciousness, I quickly grabbed my phone and frantically typed a timeline of what I'd experienced. I wanted to remember everything that had happened. The following morning, I read what I'd written in my deeply fatigued state:

Group of friends go traveling in outer Korea. Get kidnapped by evil tyrant. Tyrant makes them play ancient prison game—one of the group is killed every two days in immunity trial set up. Eventual winner is released to tell the tale. Battle of friendship.

On paper, it makes me look like I should be locked up in some sort of mental asylum. During my commute to work the next day, I couldn't stop staring at the words I had hastily written. Something seemed so familiar about them.

I was intensely obsessed with this story. The fact I'd almost convinced myself that I had actually lived through it was another matter. I'll blame the extreme wooziness for such madness.

In the days that followed, I was adding to the storyline. Out of nowhere, members of the United Nations were getting involved in subplots and the main character had a love interest within the group. It was becoming my very own book or movie.

That's when it hit me. Why don't I turn it into one? Inside one week, with a journalism degree in my back pocket, a tangle of unpaid sports and comedy writing engraved into my bow, and the fact I didn't have millions of pounds wedged under a pale, lumpy mattress to commission a Hollywood blockbuster, I plumped for the book option.

Quickly, things gathered momentum. In no time I had a full storyline and a first chapter in place. Unfortunately, due to working full time and honoring other commitments, the whole idea soon fell flat on its backside. I simply couldn't dedicate the required time and energy.

The final nail in the coffin was when I realized why the whole story seemed so familiar. In the weeks leading up to these visions, I had been reading *The Hunger Games* trilogy and caught up on the latest season of CBS' reality TV show *Survivor*. Suddenly, I saw it was no coincidence I'd been taking in these forms of media and subsequently had a dream that was basically a hybrid of both. Once that realization sank in, the shine was well and truly taken away from the whole concept.

Regardless, for the first time in as long as I could remember, I felt excited by the prospect of something. Even though my idea never got past first base, it shined a light that suggested it was possible to go one further than forever wasting away in the bowels of the advertising firm I worked for.

Whilst this light faded into the distance, I found myself sleepwalking back into my sloth-like routine. Before I knew it, six weeks had passed. I was feeling torn. The idea of writing a book continued to dangle like a carrot in front of me.

On a dark, wet and overcast Saturday, I found myself walking around the streets of my hometown. As I headed back to my apartment, I made the quickfire decision to pop into the local library. Why? I wasn't totally sure. I hadn't been to a library since I was at university, and that was never a pleasurable experience.

There's no place quite like a university library. Where else can you find hundreds of hungover people pretending to work? Plus, if you're in the wrong place at the wrong time, it's likely you'll witness some poor soul chucking up their guts into a photocopier.

"Can I help you, sir?" enquired the startled librarian.

"Ermm, nah. Having a browse thanks," I nervously replied.

She smelled my fear as I aimlessly walked in any old direction. This became apparent when I soon found myself disoriented in the prenatal aisle. During this escapade, I saw numerous book titles that I firmly believe no human's brain should ever process.

What was I doing? I detected the library regulars staring at me, sensing I didn't belong there. After ten grueling minutes, I soon plucked up the courage to move on. My pathetic attempt of surrounding myself with literature and hoping it would deliver some sort of guidance or inspiration had left me feeling nauseous. Although, I think that was more down to the horrific images on display in the prenatal section.

On my way to the exit, I wasn't finished with making a fool out of myself. Out of nowhere, I tripped over a mound of books that saw me fall to the ground. The roars of laughter that came from the regulars muffled the crashing sounds of the books. Once I got to my feet, I made a beeline for the exit.

That's when, in my peripheral vision, I saw an unbelievably familiar looking book sprawled on the ground. It was in really bad condition. If my fall hadn't disturbed the dust from the front cover, I probably wouldn't have recognized it. The book was *Up Pompey*, and was written by an American journalist called Chuck Culpepper.

Pompey is Portsmouth's nickname. A few years before, I remembered getting my dad this book for Christmas. The story revolves around how an American sports writer becomes disenchanted with covering football and baseball, so travels across the Atlantic to get a taste of the English Premier League. He followed Portsmouth around for a few months and told the tale in his book.

I'd never read it, but I'd always considered it to be a distinctive idea. It soon dawned on me that the inspiration was right here at my fingertips in the form of this shabby, relic of a book. I could do the opposite. Travel to America and write about my new favorite passion—college football.

Later in the evening, my head felt like it was spinning. The enthusiasm of that first day when I came up with the derivative Hunger Games meets Survivor idea came roaring back.

My initial concern was maybe someone had already done what I was setting out to do. Following some quick searches online, I found a couple of books that English people had written about the NFL, but not one specifically about college football. In fact, the only material I found about an Englishman's perspective on college football was a video of comedian, actor and writer Stephen Fry. He was attending the Iron Bowl in 2010. On this episode of BBC's *Stephen Fry in America*, he stated:

> *It's an indication of the size of the US economy and their passion for sports that this is the stadium of Auburn, no more than a medium sized college, and this is their annual game against another college within the same state, The University of Alabama, based in Tuscaloosa only a few hours drive away. This fixture has the scale, intensity and hoopla of a Grand National Final, but in reality is nothing more than a local derby between amateur students. Only in America.*

Throughout the three-minute video, Fry looks completely flummoxed by the whole occasion. It simply added fuel to my fire. He finished the three-minute clip by saying:

> *I really don't know if anything sums up America better. It's simultaneously preposterous, incredibly laughable, impressive, charming, ridiculous, expensive, overpopulated and wonderful.*

With each second that went by, the whole idea became more and more appealing. The only drawback I foresaw was who my target audience would be. In a country where a fourth-tier soccer match between minnows Accrington Stanley and Newport County attracts 25,000 more viewers on a Sunday than the UK's American football coverage, I felt like I could be flogging a dead horse.

Nonetheless, I was determined not to let this dream of mine fizzle out again. There was no more room for making excuses.

Once I had this vague concept set in stone, the hard work of turning it into reality was next on the agenda. As I sat down in front of the 2013 college football schedule, I circled potential games I'd love to experience. After coming up with a hypothetical itinerary, I was knocked back by how much it would all cost. Let's just say, I fully underestimated the size of America. I didn't realize that if I wanted to get to a majority of these games, I'd need to rack up thousands of air miles or take up residency in a hire car.

Without warning, I fell back to square one. On that list I couldn't stop staring at one game in particular: Alabama at Texas A&M on September 14th. It was circled an extra three times over all the other matchups.

However, with a strict and modest budget in place, it was time to lower my gaze and open myself up to cheaper, more affordable options. This pointed me in one direction—Penn State. With my family living in close proximity, it posed as the ideal destination for me to experience college football on a big scale and more importantly, it wouldn't break the bank.

During my perusal of their 2013 schedule, I was underwhelmed. Similarly, the dark cloud of the child sex abuse scandal hovered. What was the atmosphere going to be like? Did I really want to choose this place because it was the easy option?

At the back of my mind, one place nagged away at me throughout. There was just something about it that I couldn't shake. Texas A&M's tractor beam was drawing me in.

The Aggies' schedule looked favorable. They kick-started their season with four consecutive home games. After going on the road twice, they were penciled in to return to Kyle Field for another four games.

By this point I wasn't sure how long I'd spend across the pond, or if I'd stay in the same place the whole time. In an ideal world, I'd have possessed an unlimited budget that would have seen me travel the length and breadth of the country. Sadly, my name is not William Gates.

The next few days were spent thrashing out the cost of each conceivable adventure. I couldn't help but snigger to myself as I realized a few months before, I was looking to travel to College Station for a single weekend. Now, I was looking at the possibility of going there for an entire football season.

In spite of this, once I calculated how much heading to Texas would cost, I was left shuddering. In a bid to make it happen, I'd need to milk my savings dry.

Penn State was beginning to look more and more attractive by the minute. As much as A&M was the apple of my eye, from a monetary and logistical standpoint it would be difficult. But not impossible.

I ran the figures again, and again.

If I was willing to reside in the cheapest accommodations and get flights at illogical times, I could probably manage it.

At this point I concluded that if writing about A&M was achievable, I should do everything in my power to do so. The saying, "If you're going to do it, do it properly," came to mind.

From the first time I saw the Aggies play at Kyle Field, I wanted to experience it. Back then did I ever think I'd end up jumping ship to go there for several months? Not in a million years. But it felt right, and the prospect of it genuinely excited me. Penn State didn't quite have the same appeal, X factor or Johnny Manziel.

As soon as I'd made my verdict, I was all in. The path was in front of me. At last my vague objective of going to America and writing about college football wasn't just a scatterbrained idea dreamed out of the bottom of a pint glass. It had a desti-nation.

I'll be honest; the prospect of going to Texas made me equally animated, nervous and anxious. I knew next to noth-ing about the place other than a few cultural beacons such as a love for firearms, religion, cowboys and Matthew McConaughey. Moreover, I had a sizeable hunch that the JFK assassination occurred on Texan soil.

Nevertheless, I couldn't wait to get there. Going into the complete unknown whilst riding solo was something I'd never done before.

The dates were quickly put in place. I intended to fly out for the first four home games, fly back to England, and return two weeks later for the next round of games at Kyle Field.

If I had to guess, I'd say I spent roughly three straight weeks scrolling through Expedia looking for the best possible deal. It was excruciatingly painful at times, especially finding places to stay for the weekends. Everywhere seemed to double their prices on Fridays and Saturdays.

After almost losing the will to live, my index finger quiv-ered over the "Confirm Payment" button. And with one click of the mouse, I'd finally grown the balls to chase my dream.

7. WHATEVER WILL BE, WILL BE

I hadn't been this excited since I received a table for Christmas during my childhood. This wasn't any old slab of wood you'd eat your dinner off. Oh no. It was a magical, interchangeable games table that gave you the option to play pool, tenpin bowling and foosball. In a way, this gift perfectly symbolized my upcoming adventure.

Throughout my youth, every Christmas followed a similar path. My older brother, Alex, would be so excited and distracted that he'd wake me up at approximately 2:00 a.m. We'd then endure a grueling wait until my parents rose from their slumber several hours later. In this period of time, we'd be subjected to late-night television that consisted of the 24-hour news channel being on a thirty-minute loop all the way up until 6:00 a.m. It was repetitive torture.

However, one year – a game changer was introduced. Following heavy complaints from myself over this affliction, my mother agreed that when we woke up we'd be permitted to open one present each from under the tree. This was a peace offering to keep us entertained and restrain us from storming their bedroom and demanding they arise for present opening time at 4:00 a.m.

It was a masterstroke to negotiate such a deal. Unfortunately, it had a noticeable drawback. My brother failed to get to sleep at all. Before I knew it, I was trudging down the stairs with an even longer wait ahead of me. This time though, I was comforted by the knowledge that I'd soon be hearing the cackling tones of wrapping paper being torn.

I surveyed the Christmas tree like an infatuated hawk. Which one should I choose? Each gift I held instantly became my preferred choice. I repeatedly agonized over the particular one I should open. Even superstition entered my decision-making process. I ignored all of the presents that'd been wrapped in red paper. To me, red represented evil—it was the primary color of both Manchester United and Southampton Football Clubs.

Meanwhile, Alex had swiftly honed in on his choice. Before I even had time to react, he was peering down on his new, shiny, Star Trek gizmo. I'm no Trekkie, but even I could appreciate that he'd struck gold. His present of choice would occupy him for a prolonged period and see him through this cold, blustery, and long December night.

All eyes were on me. It was my turn to roll the dice. I had narrowed it down to two options. Both seemed similar in stature and had my preferred blue wrapping paper hugging each corner.

Eventually, my assessment was complete, and I was now weighing up a solitary parallelogram. As I started to tear the paper's exterior, out of nowhere something caught my eye. It was a box I'd failed to notice because it was lodged right behind the Christmas tree. I couldn't believe I'd come so close to overlooking such a menacingly wrapped structure.

It dwarfed all my other presents in size. Superstitions abruptly went out of the window. I didn't care that it was encased in devilish red paper. It was the predominant gift, so it had to be supreme, right? Alex shot me a tentative look whilst half-heartedly agreeing with my "biggest is best" policy. He knew this was a do or die moment.

I'd never felt my hands shake with such verve. This was the determining factor whether Christmas was going to be a roaring success or complete failure. What could it be? A games console? A mini soccer goal?

As the paper crumpled into my sweaty palms, the horrors of the situation soon struck. Standing before me, in all its putrid glory, was a "Where's Waldo?" board game. The words on the front of the box rapidly etched themselves into the cores of my retinas:

MINIMUM OF THREE PLAYERS REQUIRED

I tried to hide my disappointment in front of my brother. Unfortunately, my poker face was soon shattered when he noticed the rules and stipulations brought forward by the "Where's Waldo?" board game committee.

Likewise, he rubbed salt into the wound by declaring, "Ah, that's why it was stacked behind the tree. Mum probably didn't want you to open it because she knew it'd be a waste of time."

I thanked him for the clarification.

The temptation to open another began to eat away at me. What would happen if I did? Would Santa Claus never visit again? Would I be put up for adoption? Whilst watching Alex entertain himself with his fancy acquisition, I ran the idea by him as I clutched onto the idiosyncratic Waldo toy that came included in the dreaded board game.

"Do you think Mum and Dad will mind if I open another? Mine is useless."

I knew exactly what his reaction was going to be. After all, he had a proven track record of being a goody two shoes. Once at Universal Studios in Florida, we all went on the E.T. Adventure ride. Before you hop on, you are required to give your name so at the end of the ride E.T. can thank you for helping him get home. My parents and I believed it would be amusing to give the lovable alien some improper and challenging names to pronounce. Alex strongly refused to play ball, just like I knew he wasn't going to stand for my extra present request. As predicted, he shot me down in flames.

An hour later, I was struggling. I had literally spent the last thirty minutes staring at the clock, watching the second hand tick from minute to minute. During this new hobby of mine, plan B was in action. I had sneakily been acting as a drinks waiter. Alex thought I was being the best little brother in the world as I offered to refill his mug of hot tea at regular intervals. In reality, I was speeding up the process of him visiting the toilet so I could covertly open up another present in his absence.

Sooner or later, the time arrived. As he sloped off to the other side of the house, I knew I had a window of opportunity to pounce. When it came to the crunch, I bottled it. My conscience got the better of me.

Instead, I continued playing fetch with my dog and the damn plastic Waldo figure. It certainly didn't bring a tear to my eye that our cocker spaniel, Oscar, had already made progress with chewing poor Waldo's legs off.

So, where does this phantom games table come into play, and how is it related to my upcoming trip? Well, after that taxing Christmas morning it was finally time to open our other presents. Before commencing, my dad announced he needed to go out the back and retrieve something. In due course, he returned with a large cardboard box.

"This is for you, Josh," he gleefully said.

My imagination ran wild. I was mesmerized by the thought of what it might be. This was the very same feeling that I had in the pit of my stomach in the weeks and months leading up to my Texas adventure.

I had no idea what the journey would entail, whether it was going to be a trip of a lifetime or be as much of a disappointment as I felt when I saw Waldo's grinning features looking back at me.

Life is all about throwing yourself into the unknown. This large cardboard box represented that. I had absolutely no idea what it was as it came from nowhere—purely like the concept of my pending endeavors.

Once I knew what was inside the box, the excitement and anticipation grew stronger. Following this, I had to sit and watch my dad construct the table as he sipped mulled wine and stuffed his face with canapés. It presented another anxious wait, similar to the weeks and months leading up to the end of August.

I knew what I was about to embark on, but the gap between booking everything and my flight to Houston felt like a lifetime away. Just like in the old days when I wished to start playing on that legendary table, I longed to be in Aggieland already.

In the heavy and sluggish weeks leading up to my departure, it's fair to say things could have gone smoother.

The first serious aspect of my pending trip was that I had to inform my family of my decision. Little did they know this bombshell was waiting for them around the corner. I had brief chats with Katie about it. To be honest, I don't think she ever thought I'd have the guts to go through with it, so never took my musings seriously. She realized I was discontent at work, but presumed I'd soon get over it and move on to another audacious idea.

When I prepared to announce to her that my plan was in place, I was a nervous wreck. I was fully expecting glasses and plates to be tossed around the kitchen willy-nilly. With this prediction in mind, I moved the cutlery to a safe location.

Silence. I'd delivered the news. More silence. The shock reverberated around the room. After a couple of tormenting minutes, she finally spoke.

"OK, if it makes you happier than you are at the moment, then I'm fine with it. Oh, and you can bring me back a designer handbag."

I was stunned that she took it so well. It was a huge weight off my shoulders, and the fact I had her support meant a great deal. Moments later, an allowance for a handbag was swiftly added to the dwindling budget.

Next up was my mother.

With my parents living across the pond, we communicated on Skype a couple of times a week. On this day I emailed them saying I urgently needed to speak with them.

Since I'd done this a grand total of zero times before, I think my mum assumed there had been some sort of emergency. As she appeared on my grainy laptop screen, she seemed flustered and worried.

At the back of my mind, I thought if things went south, I could disconnect the internet and pretend that the conversation never happened. Luckily for me, she digested the news fine. I don't think she fully understood what I was explaining or what I was about to embark on, but when I was younger she'd always wanted me to go traveling by myself in order to gain independence and a level of exploration. She probably thought that this was a rather delayed attempt at doing so.

Moments after speaking to her, I heard my phone ringing in the other room. I went to see who it was. It was my father. Clearly, news didn't take long to travel around the Perry clan.

Frustratingly, there was a painfully large delay on the call. We were speaking over each other as I awkwardly attempted to explain why I was going to Texas. I could tell he was nowhere near as enthusiastic about it as my mum was. It was difficult to gauge his opinion as questions rained down about why I was going down this path.

I had expected a frosty reaction from him. To be honest, it didn't bother me. If anything, it spurred me on to make the most of this adventure and prove to him I wasn't simply running away. Instead, I was doing something positive and not just going on a jolly to the States for a few months to drink beer and watch football.

Although, to be fair, I intended to do my fair share of that.

Three weeks before heading to the promised land of Texas, I received some potentially devastating news. No, my passport wasn't on the brink of expiring. It was something far worse. The clock had innocently struck the daredevil time of 11:00 p.m.

I was getting ready to call it a night and turn the bedroom light off when I decided to quickly check my phone for the latest current affairs and sports news. People all over social media were going crazy over a link that directed to ESPN's homepage. As soon as the page loaded, the headline appeared:

NCAA INVESTIGATING TEXAS A&M QUARTERBACK JOHNNY MANZIEL

I nervously shrieked. Why was he being investigated? After processing the opening paragraph, my heart began to sink.

ESPN was reporting that Manziel had allegedly been paid five-figure sums of cash to sign hundreds of pieces of memorabilia. Consequently, the NCAA had launched an investigation into finding out if the reigning Heisman Trophy winner had broken strict NCAA rules that forbid collegiate players from cashing in.

If guilty, Manziel would almost certainly be ruled ineligible for the upcoming season. I couldn't believe what was happening. Johnny was one of the major reasons why I was drawn to Texas A&M and to college football as a whole. I craved to see him terrorize a team in the same way as he did in the first half of that opening SEC game against Florida—the game that put A&M on my radar.

There's nothing like watching him in his element on a football field. It was one of the things I was most looking forward to. Now, this vision was thrown into severe doubt. Understandably, I barely slept that night. I was praying it was all bluster, and that some crooked autograph brokers were cowardly out to make a quick buck at Manziel's expense.

However, I always fear the worst. In the weeks that followed, a handful more tyre kickers came to the fore with further whispers about Manziel signing memorabilia for cash.

Additionally, there were questionable images of items being signed that added fuel to the fire. By this point, I'd convinced myself that he was going to be found guilty. Texas A&M remained tight-lipped throughout, whilst every entity of ESPN seemed certain he was due for the guillotine.

I searched for comfort on Aggies' message boards, but found a world of panic. People were almost suicidal at the thought of backup, Matt Joeckel, filling Johnny's boots. I had no idea who Joeckel was, but these murmurings hardly filled me with much confidence. After looking for some reassurance, I was left feeling even more cheesed off.

With the days drawing closer to my departure, the investigation continued to rumble on. No matter how many times I checked all the latest college football sources, no one had a clue what the outcome would be.

With this in mind, I tried to gracefully look on the bright side of life. There was nothing I could do about it.

Whatever will be, will be.

8. STARING AT THE FLIGHT PATH TRACKER

The day before heading to Texas, I felt a mixture of anticipation and uneasiness. At last it had dawned on me that I was leaving my stable job, girlfriend and apartment behind to immerse myself into the unknown.

Shortly after coming up with the concept of going to America and writing about college football, I decided I wanted my adventure to be as authentic as possible.

When reading other forms of sporting literature, it was always the unexpected and unscripted moments that hit me the hardest. As far as I was concerned, the more surprises and shocks I'd be in for, the better. I was determined to head to Texas with no motives or hidden agendas. Quite simply, I was going there to write about what I saw—good or bad.

Yes, I did a little research here and there. How else would I know how to get from Houston's George Bush Intercontinental Airport to Kyle Field?

Looking at the bigger picture, I genuinely didn't have a clue what to expect. The few times I did slap "College Station" into Google brought conflicting reviews. Some were positive, including the statistic that it's the most educated city in Texas; some were negative, especially about a certain place or person called Bryan. Who or what was Bryan? I had no idea.

Likewise, there were some offbeat tidbits that claimed as long as you say, "gig 'em" and put a thumb up now and then, you'll be fine. I sat there struggling to comprehend this. I'd only used my thumb as a greeting maybe once or twice in my life, and it was probably when heavily intoxicated.

There were also some warnings. I read an extract that claimed you're not permitted to walk on a particular patch of grass. If you did, you'd find yourself in an awful lot of trouble. Where was this grass? In an attempt to not come across the College Station Police Department, I made the bizarre pledge to never walk on grass while I was out there.

Seeking further helpful advice, I visited a prestigious Aggies' website and message board called TexAgs. I wasn't prepared for what I was about to see. Heaps of people were passionately arguing the pros and cons of having a Waffle House near the university campus. At first, I thought this potato-themed abode would be a tourist attraction that would be an actual structure made out of square-shaped batter. Only later I realized it was, in fact, a popular breakfast franchise.

On the same investigatory mission, I came across a slightly unnerving article that outlined a number of reasons why you should find yourself disliking Texas A&M. The curious nature of such work got the better of me. I cautiously read it several times.

Firstly, it was clear that a supporter of the Aggies' rivals, Texas Longhorns, had written this slanderous piece. Taking this into account, I studied it with a large grain of salt. Their main gripes with A&M revolved around superficial aspects, such as the zero cheerleader policy.

However, the last paragraph did take me by surprise. It referred to something called the "jizz jar." It claimed a portion of male Aggies set their semen on fire to represent their hatred

71

for the UT Tower, whatever that was. Accompanying such allegations was a video that showed members of the A&M Corps of Cadets squeezing their genitalia during a game in a bid to share with the on-field athletes' pain. I could safely say I'd never witnessed anything like that before.

Nonetheless, I knew it was a disparaging piece designed to put A&M down. For instance, if a Portsmouth fan wrote a similar item on Southampton, they would claim their rivals regularly sleep with horses, procreate with members of their own family and posses nine nipples. It's a rivalry for a reason, isn't it?

Despite reading various outsiders' views on A&M and drawing the conclusion that this place had the potential to be monumentally different to anywhere I'd ever experienced, I remained determined to keep an open mind.

With less than twenty-four hours until my flight, my belongings were packed. I contemplated that this was perhaps the craziest thing anyone I'd ever known had done.

I considered if a friend of mine approached me and said that they were thinking of quitting their job to fly across the world for an amateur sport, I'd probably tell them to have a cold shower and book a consultation with a reputable psychologist.

And then it happened. ESPN's College Football's website slowly buffered. All I saw was the headline.

JOHNNY MANZIEL BANNED

There and then I was ready to jack it all in (the trip, not my life). I clenched onto the laptop and got ready to throw it at the wall in disgust. My throwing arm was locked halfway back until I saw in the corner of my eye, a line of words that saved me a few hundred quid. These words will stay with me forever.

"Manziel to sit out the first half against Rice."

"Half a game? Half a f***ing game!" I shouted.

I broke into song. I was delighted. For weeks I'd feared the worst. At one point it seemed unlikely I'd get to see Johnny in action at all. Now it was guaranteed.

With this news and the way it made me feel, it proved to me that I was ready and doing the right thing. Logically? It still seemed a barmy and a puzzling life path to choose. But where does logic get you? I had used logic all my life, and never in my wildest dreams did I think I'd come close to doing something like this.

The next morning, it was time to head to the airport. It was an early flight. Thanks to a mixture of anxiety, adrenaline and a fear of flying, I barely slept the night before.

After making sure I had my passport and plane tickets on me at least a dozen times, I was on my way. Figuratively speaking, the referee's whistle had just been blown to signal the kickoff of my adventure.

Once I arrived at the airport, I set about finding the departures board. My eyes scanned for Houston. I took in a deep breath as I whispered the quick prayer that everyone does at the airport: "Please don't let the flight be delayed. Oh, and I hope I'm not sitting next to Richard Reid. Amen."

Those comforting words, "On Time," graced the intimidating black monitors.

My pace quickened as I swiftly strode to the gate.

Then it hit me.

I'd almost forgotten to carry out my pre-flight ritual. For luck, I visit the cuddly, eight-foot Harrods bear that stands proudly in every English airport. After giving him a patronizing pat on the head, I was now in my element.

Operation Texas was underway.

Right before take-off, the pilot made the mandatory announcement welcoming everyone to the plane. Yawn. He then delivered the dialogue that never fails to inadvertently make me laugh. It was the usual guff about how flying conditions are looking very good and clear. It then hits you, what else is he going to proclaim? "Hi guys, I'm sorry to say the skies are looking grim at best. There's plenty of rough stuff about. If I'm being brutally honest, I'll do well to land this bird. Strap yourselves in, folks; it's going to get messy." Could you imagine that?

Houston is approximately 4,847 miles away from London. After a flight duration of ten hours and ten minutes, I was feeling numb. There becomes a stage on a journey when you genuinely lose all hope that you will ever reach your intended destination. My breaking point is usually around the seventh or eighth hour.

I'll hold my hands up and admit to being a nervous flyer, but this hasn't always been the case. In 2011, I was on a flight that changed everything. Before this escapade, flying didn't bother me. In fact, I'd go as far as saying I was good at it. I'd sleep and watch movies with real flair. Once, a complete stranger even took the time out of their busy schedule to mention that I looked at home in the clouds.

I took to flying like a duck to water. I mean, who doesn't enjoy getting drunk on mini bottles of alcohol and passing out for the rest of the flight? Granted, you will wake up with a stinking hangover, but look on the bright side, you don't have to listen to the infant three rows behind screaming because the entertainment magazine has confirmed their worst nightmare—Madagascar 3 is not part of the entertainment package.

So, why did I suddenly have the heebie-jeebies when it came to being propelled 35,000 feet into the sky? Well, let's just say the fear developed following a rather terrifying experience. I was with Katie as we flew from the Cook Islands to New Zealand.

All week leading up to the flight we had been unsure whether it would go ahead. A Chilean volcano had erupted, meaning an ash cloud dominated a large stretch of the southern hemisphere.

Hundreds of flights had been grounded. The Pacific was pretty much a dead zone for planes. On the day of the journey, we queued at a bus stop waiting to be picked up. A German couple came striding towards us.

"Don't bother! No flights will be leaving. We were on a plane yesterday and it barely got us here. There's no way they will let the planes off the runway today," they jointly claimed.

Luckily, we didn't take their advice. On our arrival at Rarotonga airport it seemed like the flight had got the all clear. We checked in without a fuss and hoped the Germans' story was vastly exaggerated.

Unfortunately, it wasn't. The journey was unpleasant, and that's being kind. For the first time in my life I thought there was a real possibility that I was going to perish. It was crazy. On this five-hour flight the early stages went fine. After that, everything went haywire.

My spider sense was tingling as we sat through a series of disconcerting turbulence. The pilot delivered a cocktail of reassurances and warned there'd likely be more bumps along the way because we were flying at less altitude to avoid the ash cloud.

Minutes later there was a twist in the tail. An airhostess came sprinting down the aisle demanding people put their seatbelts on immediately. That's never a good sign, especially as they usually walk around mumbling, "Put ya seatbelts on," in an emotionless state.

This was different. They knew a dose of brown stuff was about to hit the fan—and it did. For fifteen seconds, the plane rapidly went into freefall. Moments before, people had been laughing and going, "Ooooh!" with sarcasm at the turbulence.

Now the cabin was filled with unbearable screams. I was completely bricking it. Katie was clamping onto my arm so tight that I could barely feel the right side of my body anymore.

The next few hours were blood-curdling. Just when I thought we were through the worst of it, we dropped back into freefall. Bags fell out of overhead compartments and the traumatic screeching resumed.

With an hour to go, it calmed down. We hadn't experienced turbulence for roughly twenty minutes. I needed to get up to obtain our passports from my luggage so we could fill in our immigration forms. As I leaned over to open the bag, the nose of the plane unexpectedly felt like it had flown into a brick wall. I was thrown six rows back. After crawling back to my seat on my hands and knees, there was no way I was getting up again. I closed my eyes and prayed we'd soon land in Auckland.

Thankfully, that time eventually came. Seconds later, the pilot announced on the runway: "Well… I bet you're all glad that's over with. I certainly am."

Those words pretty much summed up the ordeal. If the pilot considered it to be bleak, it must have been serious. Unsurprisingly, our flight was the last to leave the Cook Islands until the ash cloud had fully disintegrated.

The next day I was seriously looking into applying for New Zealand citizenship. As far as I was concerned, there was no way I was ever going to set foot on a plane again. That outlook didn't last long. Forty-eight hours later, we were due to fly home. Mercifully, not via the Pacific.

Putting some casual near-death experiences to one side, planes are mysterious objects. They are a diverse setting like no other. Where else in society do you enter somewhere and partake in a "walk of shame" as you stroll past a buffet of rich people in business class? You can feel their eyes burning into your soul. Plus, if you listen carefully, you can often hear a chorus of tutting and multi-millionaires exclaim, "Do they really let these peasants on planes? They don't look like they've washed in months!"

It's equally humiliating as it is impressive. You walk down the aircraft in awe. They have beds to sleep on? Effin' beds? I'm going to have to spend the next ten hours folded like a taco, and they get their own personal boudoir?

You try and hold the emotion in. Remain calm and stay strong. The last thing you want to do is show these champagne quaffing bastards a weakness. Otherwise, they'll have you over a wine barrel as they spank your naked bottom.

Who would have ever predicted that planes would replace the Roman Colosseum? Boeing 747s have suddenly become amphitheatres for the rich and famous to watch normal folk scurry into the section of the plane that's affectionately known as "Cattle Class." Oh yes, the big CC. Airlines can tart it up as much as they want by calling it "Economy," but deep down we all know the reality of the situation. This is a place where only the bravest flight attendants roam. On a good day, you might get fed the lukewarm leftovers of business class. Otherwise, it's almost certain that a combination of dog meat, barely harvested potatoes and sewage will adorn your soggy, cardboard trough.

Man, it sucks. The worst thing is if you're sitting in close proximity to the wealthy lot. If you get up for a leak, you must try your hardest not to look in their direction. Even a quick glimpse at their set-up can automatically place you into a world of depression.

I'm weak though—I can't help myself. On one loathsome flight, I tripped over an elderly woman's moldy sandal that was dripping in a clear, damp residue. After nearly gagging, I reached the curtain of dejection and peered around the screen that separated heaven and hell. I almost fainted with ecstasy. The atmosphere could not have been more different. The air was filled with the effervescent smell of happiness. In every direction there was something wonderful. If it wasn't a sexy airhostess in six-inch killer heels or a juicy tender pork chop, it was those damn beds. They were taunting me. My spine cried out as it dealt with the realization that I'd soon be climbing back into my region of doom.

Apart from your back feeling like it's going to break into a million pieces, do you know what's even more painful? When you've had a taste of the big time. Yes, that's right. On one glorious occasion in the past, I convened with the bourgeoisie.

'What? I thought you were all about power to the people? An everyman!'

That is indeed the case. But if someone waves a free upgrade at you, I don't care who you are; you're going to snap their hand off.

The wheels were in motion. I'd soon be seated amongst individuals that brush their teeth with caviar and possess a hotline to the royal family. I was a little nervous. In advance of getting on the jumbo jet, we were meant to congregate at something that was being billed as a lounge.

My immediate thought was maybe this was some kind of vetting process designed to weed out the people that didn't belong in business class. On my approach to this darkly lit location, my breathing became intermittent. Luckily, I snapped out of it.

"Your name?" asked the female receptionist.

"Bond. James Bond," I thought I'd kick things off with a little humor as I swiveled a cocktail umbrella in the corner of my mouth. It didn't go down well. A frown saturated her face. I nervously laughed. You could have cut the tension with a knife. However, knives aren't permitted in airports.

"Sorry... Perry. Josh Perry. F***. Simply Josh Perry."

By this point I was all over the place. She ended up taking pity and allowing me entry. Just.

As I joined the rich dudes and dudettes, I took in my surroundings. Very plush. Before I knew it, I had a glass of exclusive champagne in one hand and a copy of a men's lifestyle magazine in the other.

Don't get me wrong; I wasn't about to throw all of my morals away, because I was now experiencing a thin slice of paradise. My heartstrings pulled as I imagined my fellow bros and hoes out in the terminal eating ham sandwiches and watching the departure board as a form of entertainment.

I had come a long way though. It's fair to say that I had earned my upgrade. Whether it was a computer error or not is still up for debate, but screw it, everyone deserves a day in the sun now and then.

To be fair, I had decided I wasn't going to play any part in the infamous "walk of shame." I was going to get on the plane as late as possible so I didn't have to witness such a punishing and disgraceful event.

Whilst the airline called out for business class, I sat at the gate patiently. Regardless, my left leg was twitching. It wanted a piece of the pie. No, I wasn't going to give in. I knew first hand how demeaning it is for people walking past those lucky select few. I was determined not to be a part of it.

Two minutes later, I found myself gargling expensive whisky as I sat with my feet up in a reclined position of luxury. In the background a harem of ultra hot airhostesses were handing out the *Daily Telegraph* and *Financial Times* broadsheet newspapers.

In the moments I wasn't checking the stock markets, I was wailing with laughter at the inelegant scruff pots and swamp donkeys that scuttled past with their tacky duty-free bags full of tobacco and the latest "smells like piss" fragrance from an American Idol runner up.

Right before my own eyes, I'd thrown all of my principles to one side in favor of truffles, lobsters and a seat that if reclined, doesn't crush a pair of frail knees.

In spite of this, throughout the flight I soon came to my senses. The food menu informed me that we'd be served medium-rare steak alongside "pommes frites." Now, I can't claim to speak fluent French, but even I guessed this was a veiled effort at making chips (fries) sound luxurious.

For some unknown reason, I found this rebranding attempt infuriating. Once these fancy potato oblongs had been placed in front of me, I started to long for my local fish and chips shop back home in Guildford.

I didn't want this grouping of upmarket congealed spuds. That's when it hit me. You can take the man out of the chippy, but you can't take the chippy out of the man.

During my flight to Houston, though, I'd have happily given my right leg for a steak and barrel full of pommes frites. As food was being handed out, the tired and uninterested airhostess delivered nine words that sent a shockwave through our entire row.

"Sorry, but we've only got the vegetarian option left."

When you find yourself watching the flight path tracker for two consecutive hours, you know you're struggling. At some stages I was convinced that the plane wasn't actually moving.

The only aspect softening the blow was the fact I was sitting in a position of power: the aisle seat. This spot of authority is very much underrated. Not only do you get to control the bladders of the people that sit between you and the window, you also have the option to dangle a leg out to trip passers by.

I don't consider myself to be a petty man, but if you're seated in front of me and fully stow your seat back for the entire flight, we're going to have issues, especially when I'm 6' 4" and have approximately one centimeter of legroom. Furthermore, I'd be surprised if anyone in the history of time has told a member of their friends or family, "You know what I'd love on this flight? I'd love if the person in front could put their headrest on my lap for the next ten hours."

Well, that's exactly what I had to endure.

So, Mr. Ten-Hour Recline, the minute you slump out of your seat and walk in a dazed and drunken state to the toilet, and I choose to lazily throw out an ankle for you to tumble over, you can save your complaints for someone that's not suffering from serious muscle cramps and the tentative early signs of deep vein thrombosis.

Unfortunately, I hadn't foreseen him tripping and nose-diving into the surgically enhanced chest of a nearby snoozing, middle-aged woman. This enraged the sleeping beauty. As I was wearing headphones, I couldn't tell for sure, but it sounded like this new character that had entered the scene hurled some incessantly harsh words in the direction of the reclining moron.

Before I processed the likelihood of a sexual assault charge being distributed, the pilot announced we were beginning our descent. Finally, Houston was in our sights.

After exiting the plane, the first realization that struck me was clear. The heat. In my rush to get all of my stuff packed, I hadn't given what I'd worn on the plane much thought. It would be the first and last time I'd wear denim in the insufferable Houston humidity.

Once I'd sweated the veggie option from my hips, I found myself in the wonderful immigration queue. Now in Europe, these things are different—very different. Essentially, all you need to do is smile and wave your passport in the general direction of someone that is ambiguously associated with the airport and you'll be let into the country on a red carpet.

In the United States of America? Oh no. A seriously different outcome should always be anticipated. On a previous trip to the US, an officer lost his temper with me because my fingerprints weren't showing up on his designated panel. I was only 13 or 14 years old, but it didn't stop him from shouting: "Come on! We haven't got all day, you know?" It has stayed with me ever since. Now as I offer up my prints, I quiver into a man that I'm far from proud of.

Previous trips to America had usually seen me traveling to destinations that are considered popular tourist locations. As much as I tried to convince myself, I didn't think they'd buy into College Station being advertised in vacation magazines across the pond, especially not with this alleged Bryan place/character knocking about. Furthermore, I was unsure whether they were going to believe I'd traveled all that way solely for college football. The queue was massive. And when I say massive, I mean it took almost two hours to greet the immigration officer that was going to settle my fate.

For the US citizens? Not a queue in sight. Pop on through; go and enjoy yourselves. Nine out of ten officers were assigned to that side of the building. Don't get me wrong, I'm not complaining. US citizens should have priority. It's their country after all. However, I've always been led to believe that the UK and US enjoy a special relationship. How about this is proven by inserting a mischievous "US and Friends... *cough* UK" line into the mix?

During this agonizing wait I found myself getting more and more anxious with each minute that went by. Also, I had to listen to a "Welcome to America" jingle and watch the video that accompanied it at least 765 times. One aspect that did cheer me up was a person in this broadcast was wearing a t-shirt that brandished, "I love London" across it. In hindsight, this probably isn't the best way to advertise your country to newcomers with the names of cities that are a long way away. At least it delivered some national pride.

Following an arduous wait, it was time. I nervously approached the immigration officer. My hand was trembling as I passed over my valid travel documents.

"Purpose of visit?"

"Erm, college football," I muttered.

"You a horn?"

"A what?" I began to panic. At first, I thought he'd asked if I was horny. I quickly realized how ridiculous that would've been.

"A Longhorn? Texas Longhorns?" he followed up.

"Ohhhh! No! I'm here for the Aggies."

"Enjoy Johnny Football."

And that was that. Panic over. I was in.

My initial priority was finding Terminal C. According to my scrappy piece of paper, this was where the College Station shuttle picks you up from. I soon found an almost comical monorail that takes you there. It was a Disney World-esque experience, but a hundred times more disappointing, as there was no Magic Kingdom or Epcot at the end of it.

In its place, there was a nerve-racking wait for a shuttle I prayed would take me to the promised land of Aggie football. As my pick-up time approached, I naturally proceeded to worry. I had terrible flashes that I was at the wrong terminal / booked the wrong dates / no shuttle even existed.

Alas, after some squeaky bum time, a representative from the exceptional Ground Shuttle Company came to my rescue. They saw the panic and confusion etched across my features and enquired if I fancied going to Aggieland. Needless to say, I bloody did.

So, off we went on our joyous travels. On this trek into the heart of Texas, I was understandably animated. All I wanted to do was chant fight songs, sing about Johnny Manziel and drink cheap American lager from stereotypical red cups. Even though I had been awake for 26 straight hours, I was more than ready to turn it into a fun bus.

Regrettably, my compadres inside the van were having none of it. They were four, ultra serious Chinese scholars. Silence. I zipped my face as I watched these chaps prepare for their punishing academic studies. They weren't totally mute. One of the guys did confirm that if he failed the upcoming semester, his father would lodge a set of bagpipes up his rectum. I soon sympathized with their lethargic antics. I ended the debacle by wishing them well.

Throughout the journey we turned off the highway and went past somewhere that I can only describe as a gothic, garden ornament empire. I'd never seen anything like it. On this bend of road there were hundreds, maybe thousands, of concrete garden features. They ranged from mini statues of Jesus to highly advanced frogs that counted fishing as an everyday hobby. Regardless, I felt like we were getting closer to a place that the driver had affectionately labeled, "C-Stat."

I soon recognized the names of human settlements. For example, we drove through a region called Navasota. I'd looked at getting a hotel there for the Alabama weekend in my desperate time of need.

I'll be honest; I was apprehensive when I saw the look on the driver's face as I delivered the name of the venue I was due to spend the next few months in. When I booked my accommodation, I only had two images that were on their website to go on. They looked satisfactory, but when I looked on Google Maps a few days later, I was slightly horrified by what I saw. Then again, I was reassured by the fact their brightly lit sign outside reception had two palm trees displayed.

As we parked up, I came to the resounding conclusion: it could be worse. Plus, I was too tired to care anyway. All I wanted to do was get into bed, have a wonderful night's sleep and wake up with College Station as my oyster.

Unfortunately, things didn't exactly pan out this way. To my surprise, there was a queue to check-in. Two peacekeepers from Qatar were chatting to the receptionist. I stood there for what seemed an eternity. By this point I was shattered to the extreme. In fact, looking back, it might have quite possibly been the first time in my life where I fell asleep standing up.

Off the back of a draining wait, it was finally my turn to be allowed access to the building. I simply wanted the key and the ability to go on my merry way. Two words. Wishful thinking.

"Oh my God, you're British!" exclaimed the receptionist. I weakly nodded.

"London 2012 was the most amazing spectacle ever. Tell me all about it!"

For the next fifty-five minutes, I had to give my personal blow-by-blow account of the Olympics. The irony was that it was the exact same experience she had. Like her, I was seated on my couch for the entirety of it. And yet, that didn't seem to matter. Medal tables, future hosts and Usain Bolt's yellow sneakers were all discussed at length.

Towards the end of the conversation, I was made to feel particularly embarrassed. She asked if I had been to Texas before and if I had any knowledge of the area. Of course, I didn't have much to contribute. This still didn't stop me from delving into the depths of my overtired brain to uncover something impressive to say. As this was happening, two subjects kept swirling around my wearied head—the popular 90's Scottish band, Texas, and Whitney Houston. Now, I know what you're probably thinking, Whitney Houston? Apart from her surname, what exactly has she got to do with Texas? The answer is simple: nothing. That shows how much I was thrashing about. Eventually, I threw NASA out there. It seemed to get me off the hook.

She was the first person I'd met in Aggieland, and I could already tell this place was unusual. Even though at the time I didn't particularly welcome the conversation because of exhaustion, she had a warmness that meant I couldn't help but give her the time of day. I walked away from that initial meeting thinking, well, that would never happen at home!

Ultimately, I found my way to my room. Whilst devouring a tuna melt that I'd acquired from a nearby Jimmy John's sandwich shop, I flicked on the television. I was relieved not to have a trace of British pop culture stand before me. Instead, I fell asleep to the soothing sights and sounds of the Dallas Cowboys playing the Houston Texans in an NFL preseason game accompanied by Spanish commentary. Bloody delightful.

9. An Unforgettable Midnight

Whilst the sunlight blazed through the single-glazed windows, I courageously shook off the wilting signs of jet lag and came to my senses. I was here. I'd made it.

After traveling 5,000 miles the day before, it was tempting to lie in bed forever. The unforgiving Texas sun had other ideas. As it sliced beyond the worn and shabby curtains, I grew familiar with what would become my unknowing alarm clock for the next few months. I was feeling a heavy dose of enthusiasm and apprehension. I needed beer. It was 5:47 a.m.

Getting ready felt strange. What does an Englishman wear in 100 degrees? It's considered a grandiose achievement if the British Isles gets visited by the sun more than ten times a year, let alone deal with soaring temperatures that pose a potential health risk. Following some careful consideration, I applied two gallons of sunblock.

At last I was ready to explore Aggieland on foot. Yes, that's right, due to my modest budget; my mode of transportation was to be my trusty legs. There'd be no luxurious hire car on this rodeo.

Ten minutes later, I found myself strolling down South Texas Avenue in the direction of the university campus. I'd only walked fifty yards and had already proceeded to sweat profusely. The humidity was choking me. I desperately needed water. Where could I get some? I had zero knowledge of the area and it wasn't even 6:30 a.m. yet. Would anywhere even be open? I'd been in the Brazos Valley barely five minutes and I was already floundering.

In the back of my mind, I prayed this wasn't a sign of things to come. It was a lesson that I needed to learn quickly. I couldn't simply resort to autopilot like I did back home. Why? Because I'm familiar with the norms of my usual surroundings. Here, I had no idea. I was going to have to learn as I went along. Eventually, I was able to source some soothing H2O and stay alive—for now.

I'd soon get used to the long stretch of South Texas Avenue. It was my tunnel to the fruits of College Station. That first day I walked, walked and walked some more. As I passed parking lots, gas stations and a wide array of shops, I took in the fresh morning air. Butterflies continued to flutter inside my stomach as I negotiated with the fact this would be my home until the wintery months.

Before I dwelled on such realizations for much longer, I began to observe the finer details. There was a recurring theme throughout. The Texas A&M logo. It was here, there and everywhere. In one instance, a hamburger restaurant displayed it with more prominence over their company logo. Straight off the bat, I detected this place revolved around one characteristic—the university.

Once I arrived at this conclusion, I saw a monster purring in the distance. This gargantuan structure lay flat on the horizon, dwarfing everything in its vicinity. My first sighting of the eighth wonder of the world. Kyle Field.

Immediately, like a fly to a light bulb, I was drawn to it. In all the weeks leading up to arriving in Aggieland, I hadn't imagined the campus, Northgate, or my charming, one-star travel tavern. Oh no, I had pictured myself watching Johnny Manziel throwing touchdown passes to Mike Evans at the Mecca of Aggie football.

The frequency of my strides increased. Realistically, I was still a couple of miles away, but I had my target in sight and no one was going to stop me. I wanted my first taste of Aggie football as quickly as possible.

Forgetting the intensity of the sun, I soon had to stop and reacquaint myself with my new, trusted best friend: a cheeky bottle of water. I felt like a car. I'd walk a few hundred yards, then have to stop to fill up. It was nauseating, but essential.

Sooner or later, the strenuous journey came to an end. The colossus that is Kyle Field stood before me. Its sheer presence conveyed the history and atmosphere of Texas A&M. Even at such an early stage, I firmly believed I'd chosen to come somewhere special.

I ended up walking around the stadium multiple times. I needed to get my bearings. After all, I'd be back in less than twenty-four hours for the 2013 season opener against Rice University.

In fact, I'd actually be back sooner. From the very first time I'd discovered Texas A&M, I had known about the midnight yell practices that take place on the nights before each football game at Kyle Field. However, a couple of weeks before I arrived in Texas, I noticed there was a concert scheduled for the 13th September (the night before the Alabama game). This was being billed as the "First Yell." As a naive gentleman, I took this at face value and presumed I'd have to wait until then to experience my first taste of yell practice. Luckily, I soon discovered this was not the case.

Following a day of exploration, I finally cooled off with the beer I'd been craving since half past five in the morning. I found myself at Sully's Sports Grill & Bar. As soon as I glanced at my phone, I noticed the soccer European Super Cup had kicked off. English club, Chelsea, was battling it out with the Germans in the form of Bayern Munich.

After a couple of minutes I realized the chances of them showing soccer were slimmer than Miley Cyrus. I nervously approached the bar. Happily, I didn't find Miss Cyrus there.

"Can you put the soccer on?" I enquired. I was greeted with blank looks. My accent had just confused the first of countless Texans.

Once an exuberant sauce called Ranch had been sampled, I was blessed with a thin slice of home. Needless to say, I was the only person in this place watching soccer. Who could blame them? There were 54 other HDTVs to choose from. It was like a sports cornucopia with beer and waffles. A couple of hours later, my English compatriots had lost on penalties. This was a scenario I was more than used to.

I moved on. The natural question to that statement is, where? I had nowhere to go, and even more embarrassingly, nowhere in mind apart from a depressing stroll back to my uninspiring living quarters.

Ultimately, I made the verdict to head back to Kyle Field. When I was there earlier in the day I noticed plenty of people setting up for the next day's tailgating action. I figured there was a good chance some students might still be knocking about in the mood to tolerate an Englishman that was so far out of his depth it would perhaps seem sophisticated.

The moment I arrived at the stadium it swiftly became apparent that I wasn't in luck. It was a ghost town. Well, apart from a group of exceptionally drunk folk who were throwing a Frisbee at each other from five yards apart. The crowds from earlier had disappeared.

Not ideal, but I hadn't marched all that way to slope back empty handed. I decided I'd catch a glimpse of Kyle Field under the lights. I paced around to the entrance and noticed a group standing by the side of the field. I went over to have a quick chat, but was intercepted by a couple of security guards. They immediately asked what I was up to.

"Having a look around," I sheepishly responded.

Their faces dropped. For a moment I thought they were under the impression I was being rude. I repeated myself, followed with the back-story of why I was there. Luckily for me, they were two of the nicest people I'd ever met. Often when you hear about Texas, you hear about how friendly the people are. These two chaps, Jeff and Tommy, typified this and were genuinely warm-hearted towards me. I was humbled.

Whilst kibitzing, I was able to gain an extended understanding of Kyle Field's history and the planned redevelopment. For one, I couldn't believe they were making this almighty theatre even bigger! It was already the same size as England's international soccer stadium, Wembley. In a couple of years it would hold 102,000 people.

I was then informed that the population of College Station is estimated to be 97,000. I'm no mathematician, but I think I can safely conclude that means everyone in the neighborhood will be able to comfortably fit into the new stadium with room to spare.

Once I'd come to terms with that, I got to hear some humorous stories surrounding the antics students' pull to try and get onto the field. Let's just say, the 50-yard line is a rather desired destination for intoxicated couples…

The best was yet to come. Jeff and Tommy informed me that a midnight yell practice was taking place in a few hours. Furthermore, they had hooked me up with a pitch side pass for this wonderfully unique tradition. I'd get the perfect view to see it all unfold.

My mood continued to change. Throughout the day I had tried to put the complexity and reality of what I was doing to the back of my mind. Nonetheless, doubts still lingered. As inspiring as my first impressions of Aggieland were, a whole football season seemed like an awfully long time. Equally, that evening I felt relatively lonely after speaking to friends and family as I aimlessly walked around somewhere that was completely foreign to me.

What happened next changed everything. I heard a faint tune playing in the distance. It grew louder and louder with each second that went by. Sooner or later, the Fightin' Texas Aggie Band emerged from the opposite corner of Kyle Field. I was fixated. The Aggie War Hymn reverberated. It somehow made me put all my worries to one side and focus on how lucky I was to be there in that moment. It sounds crazy, but even though I was on the other side of the world from the cobbled streets of Guildford, I felt at home. There is something indescribable about the band. When they play, you feel good about yourself. It's an enigma that I wouldn't be able to put my finger on for the entire time I was in College Station. I adored it; it was the perfect start to a midnight I'll never forget.

Over the next few months there would be numerous occasions I'd describe as, "You have to see it, to believe it." This was the first of dozens.

Midnight yell practice is spine tingling. I still couldn't believe that 30,000 people gather at midnight on a Friday to practice songs for the next day's game. I was rapidly sensing the community of the university revolved around the football team like a heartbeat.

My jaw was literally on the floor. Coming from England, this was difficult to comprehend. If thousands of people got together on a Friday night back home, you could bet a fair amount of money that hundreds of police would need to be present. Paralytic lunatics would be fighting all over the place in a scene of sheer mayhem. Here though, the naughtiest thing I witnessed was two girls arguing over how many years their respective fathers had served in the military.

Even when the crowds were pouring in, I didn't believe anywhere near the projected 30,000 would turn up. I certainly had egg on my face as soon as the whole student side filled up with moments to spare.

During this tradition, not only do they rehearse fight songs, but they also jest about the next day's opposition. In this instance, A&M was playing the Rice Owls. Early on, the announcer exclaimed: "What's the difference between Rice and Cheerios? You can find Cheerios in a bowl." I guffawed.

The very second the gates opened I couldn't help but notice a large string of skinhead chaps run to the front of the bleachers. In Europe, if I saw 100 skinheads run towards me, I'd be running as fast as I could in the other direction. Why did every single one of them have no hair? Why were they wearing army gear? I turned to Jeff and asked who they were, and he replied: "The Corps." At that moment in time, those two words meant little. I weakly nodded and pretended like I understood.

The skinheads weren't the only aspect I had a hard time of getting to grips with. As I stood on the side of the pitch, I was struck by the yell leaders' actions. I had seen them on TV, but had no actual knowledge of what they did. Following a few sequences, I quickly grasped their purpose. They relayed the yells to the 12th Man via a set of special routines. Phew, I didn't have to ask Jeff another silly question. After all, I was already too embarrassed to enquire why people were hissing every so often and why when the floodlights went out; numerous people snogged each other's faces off.

At first I found the whole experience crazy—almost insane. I stood ten feet from a group in army uniforms doing press-ups and sit-ups pitch side just because people in the crowd had waved some sort of gesture at them. Likewise, there were blokes wearing dungarees chasing and rugby tackling each other on the field. The icing on the cake was when I saw someone dressed as Winnie the Pooh standing in the front row.

Soon enough, I was even more dumbfounded. For a brief moment I thought Kyle Field was under attack. I heard what sounded suspiciously like the detonation of a small bomb. Had I arrived in Baghdad by accident? It was only once I noticed everyone start to cheer that I felt reassured. Either people were celebrating the fact we were under attack, or it was merely something that usually happened and I wasn't privy to it yet. Luckily, it was the latter. I soon discovered A&M students had found a cannon in a ditch on the campus and naturally put two and two together, and integrated it into the Kyle Field experience. I bowed in amazement.

It wasn't until the next day that everything made complete sense. The unison of the crowd makes the A&M student section the best in college football. Across the pond you don't get to appreciate much of the fan-involvement. All you get to witness is what the TV networks decide to show.

The yell practices orchestrate every last detail. Everyone gets to know exactly how to make the Aggie atmosphere so special. And trust me, special is exactly what it is.

It was the perfect ending to my first day in Aggieland. Yes, I had a couple of hiccups here and there, but if midnight yell was an indication of things to come, boy was I going to love this place.

10. INITIATION

With each minute that went by, one thing was becoming clearer and clearer. College football isn't just a sport or hobby to the people of Texas; it's a religion. Even though it was the early hours of Saturday morning, I could feel it in the air—this was holy day.

I didn't sleep much after sampling the incredible scenes of midnight yell. Adrenaline was coursing through my veins. Had I really just experienced that? I came to terms with the possibility it was a jet lag induced hallucination.

Regardless, in less than eleven hours I'd be back at Kyle Field for their midday season opener against Rice University. With the early kickoff in mind, I set my alarm for some ridiculous hour. I was in no mood to oversleep. After all, it was 100 degrees outside, so if I were late there would be no chance of rushing to the stadium without suffering a serious cardiac arrest.

Alas, my trusty body clock prospered and I was awake an hour before I had originally scheduled to rise from my slumber. Once I had slapped on a generous serving of sunblock, I was good to go.

As I walked down South Texas Avenue, I sensed a distinctive atmosphere. Something felt different compared to my previous day's ramblings. In the short time I'd been here, I already considered it to be one of the most positive and happiest places I'd ever visited. Therefore, when *The Daily Beast* announced a survey that ranked the top 20 happiest colleges in America, it didn't surprise me in the slightest that Texas A&M ranked as numero uno.

On this occasion it was even more upbeat. During my voyage to find breakfast, I almost impaled myself on an Aggie flag that was stuck in the ground. Dozens of others aligned the road. Flags were everywhere, from fluctuating out of fast food outlet windows to hanging out of cars. It was clear that the whole society was buzzing for some Aggie football, and so was I.

Another feature I couldn't fail to notice was literally everyone was wearing maroon. Yet again, I stuck out like a sore thumb. Similarly, I was the only person not wearing a cap. Back in England, a cap is never considered as a necessity. In a bid to correct this, I dived into a marquee that was selling an insane amount of A&M merchandise. They had everything from golf bags to dog toys. Whilst taking an interest in a nearby selection of hats, an eager assistant approached me.

"Howdy! Y'all looking for a new lid?"

I literally had no idea what he meant. My response was embarrassing. Words deserted me as I tried to muster up the courage to enquire what a lid was. Instead, a set of deformed words exited my mouth. It had escalated into an awkward situation reminiscent of the time Katie scrolled through our deleted TV content and came across the Victoria's Secret Fashion Show.

It came as no surprise when the assistant briskly fled the scene. The look on his face suggested that I must have been from another planet. In a state of panic, I picked up the first cap I set eyes on and doubled it up with a new prim and proper maroon t-shirt that adorned Coach Sumlin's famous catchphrase, "Yes Sir." I exited before "Lid-Gate" further haunted me.

Now, I know what many of you are thinking. I've just committed a cardinal sin by turning into the stereotypical t-shirt fan. On one hand, you have a valid point. I had no connection to Texas A&M, and the only time I'd ever seen the Aggies play was on a beautiful piece of technology that's formally known as the television. That there is the sole definition of a t-shirt fan.

However, I was hardly going into this experience actively looking to become a diehard Aggie. As much as the traditions and watching Johnny Manziel play appealed to me, the fact I wasn't a current or former student of the university remained.

Did I believe there was a possibility of becoming a fully-fledged supporter in the future? Who knows? Even after such early experiences, this place was already beginning to tug at my heartstrings.

In spite of everything, I knew first and foremost I was here as a writer. I contemplated this as I found myself deep-rooted in a popular breakfast outlet called Denny's. I'd experienced this food franchise a couple of years before whilst stopping over in Los Angeles. The L.A. version made the College Station one look like a Hard Rock Café. I must admit it's a surprise I rolled the Denny's dice again following what I'd seen on the West Coast. If you enjoy dining with people that parade their gunshot wounds and men dressed as women, I'd highly recommend eating at the one next to LAX.

Irrespective of past experiences, I took on a meal that was labeled "The Lumberjack Slam." Yes, it was as brutal as it sounds. After demolishing the two sausages, two rashers of bacon, two pancakes, two eggs (sunny side up), fried potatoes and four slices of toast, I quickly departed with my pride intact.

There she was in the distance. A humming Kyle Field. As I walked in her direction, I quickly found myself surrounded by Aggies that could barely hide their pre-match excitement.

Every few seconds they let out a loud "WHOOP!"

Following a few sequences, I grew in confidence and thought I'd join in. Unfortunately, my voice does not possess the high-pitched tone needed to make the "WHOOP" sound natural. Instead, I sounded like a bloated lesbian. I cringed and pretended that I was fooling around. Deep down, I knew I wasn't. I was a sham.

In light of this, I couldn't help but notice a number of planes circling the area. They were flying adverts and banners around the sky. This would be the first of many things I hadn't seen at a sporting event. Before I sampled the other instances, there was something far more serious gaining my attention. The heat. It was registered at 102 degrees.

On my way to section 100 on the West 1st Deck, I noticed I was going to be getting the full brunt of the sun for the next three hours. Without hesitation, I made my way to the back of the stand to hang out in the shade until kickoff. I then proceeded to buy two bottles of water for $10. A ridiculous amount of money for water, but when it's the difference between life and death, I think $10 can be seen as a drop in the ocean. I completed the uneasy transaction. By the time the game finished, the second bottle tasted like bath water.

Luckily, what lay before me took my focus away from the soaring temperatures. Everything about Kyle Field on a game-day captivates you. Before I knew it, the words, "HOWDY AGGIELAND, WELCOME TO THE SEC," boomed out of the speakers.

Following this, memorable Aggie highlights were shown in a bid to get everyone pumped up for the players' entrance. In this moment I noted the structure of Kyle Field was strikingly similar to Heinz Field. With three huge sides, it has an open end that acts as a home for the impressively large screen.

People around me were going absolutely nuts as the infamous "March of Honor" got underway. This went on to become one of my favorite gameday traditions. Hearing the opening beats of the band members' drums lets you know it's time to start waving your towel in an erratic fashion. Behind the drumline comes the coaching staff and players. Throw a B-17 World War II bomber plane and a Kanye West song into the mix (yep, strange combination) and Kyle Field erupts as the Aggies take to the field.

The moment the game kicked off, I was swiftly reminded of the cannon's existence. Needless to say, it provided me with another close call of accidentally dislodging some brown stuff. In the seconds it took to compose myself, I deliberated further into the cannon's history. Where does it end? What is next going to be found in a ditch on campus? Machine gun? Nuclear warhead? After all, a cannon is not the most intimidating or scariest form of weaponry by any means. I'm no nautical expert, but isn't the cannon utilized to sink ships? By the way, such knowledge stems from watching *Pirates of the Caribbean* a couple of times. If I'm wrong, which I probably am, it won't be the first time a movie has supplied me with false information.

In this surreal moment of finally experiencing college football, I took a moment to take it all in. For months I had been imagining what it would be like. So far, it had lived up to every sky-high expectation.

The game itself flew by as Ricky Seals-Jones punched in a mazy 71-yard touchdown. Even with the roasting temperatures, the intensity on the field skyrocketed. With Johnny Manziel sitting out the first half due to his autograph-induced ban, Matt Joeckel was playing at quarterback for the Aggies. Despite not having their primary signal caller for the first thirty minutes of the match, A&M was still installed as heavy favorites to win. Therefore, it was a minor shock that the Aggies took until the second quarter to take the lead.

For a little while I considered the unthinkable could happen. Those thoughts swiftly vanished as the main man took his position under center for the second half. Johnny Football had entered the building, and what an entrance it was. Every single Aggie rose as chants of "Johnny! Johnny! Johnny!" rang around the famous stadium. As overwhelmed and elated as I was to witness one of my favorite sportsmen in the flesh, bizarrely my first thought was, *Holy smokes, his feet are bloody massive!*

Johnny saluted the student section. It was a beautiful moment that was almost enough to bring a tear to the eye. Opportunely, as I was so dehydrated, my body wasn't in the mood to give up any unnecessary H2O.

Away from Mr. Manziel, I loved the bruising nature of the A&M running backs. Tra Carson represented a battering ram as he dominated the red zone with two hard fought touchdowns. He distinctly reminded me of the ex-Steelers running back, Jerome Bettis. His bones looked like they were made out of indestructible steel. His foil, Ben Malena, also impressed me. Malena was more nimble and made the occasion look effortless as he accumulated 140 all-purpose yards without breaking a sweat.

Off the field, so many aspects of the gameday experience threw me off balance. This was a world away from any sporting event I'd previously attended. For starters, late in the first quarter I quickly learned that swearing at a college football game is an almighty faux pas.

At soccer games, the language used by a majority of the crowd is appalling. There won't be a second that goes by when you don't hear someone hurl a spate of shocking abuse in the direction of an opposition player or fan. Likewise, you get more classy exclamations such as, "Oi! Di**head! I've banged your wife!"

Now, I can't say I brought anything as top shelf as that to the ears of the former students and families sitting in my vicinity at Kyle Field, but it sure felt like I had. When I'm at a sports match, all of my inhibitions reset to default. As a result, it's apparently unacceptable to shout, "F***ing tackle the bastard!" as a Rice running back breeches the Aggies defensive line.

The reactions of the people around me suggested I'd just done something truly horrendous, like taken a picture in public with an iPad or strolled around the Memorial Student Center with my newly acquired lid on.

In this small area of discomfort, I couldn't help but chuckle to myself. At a soccer ground I'd probably get rapped on the knuckles for being too polite in my attempted outcry.

Soccer and college football fans are poles apart. For example, during the first half a Rice player went down injured and had to be cared for by the medical staff. Immediately, the stadium fell silent as players from both teams took a knee and visibly prayed for the unfortunate chap.

It made me ponder about similar scenarios inside English stadiums. Well, there would be no silence or praying for a start. Instead, you'd hear chants such as, "Let him die; let him die," and a dodgy bloke attempting to play the sound of an ambulance on an old shrieking bugle in the background.

There is very little empathy. This is magnified when the officials come into the equation. Back in 2005, one of soccer's most highly rated referees, Anders Frisk, announced his immediate retirement after officiating a Champions League match between Chelsea and Barcelona. Why? Because in the aftermath of the game in which Frisk sent off a Chelsea player, fans of the London club had been sending death threats to his family via voicemails, emails and letters.

The worrying thing is, even though this was one of the most high profile examples, they happen almost every week. A few more crazy stories include a Swiss official called Urs Meier. He was the victim of a hate campaign in the wake of disallowing a last-minute England goal at Euro 2004. This incident was unique, because the agenda wasn't driven by fans, but from the national media. Various UK newspapers went as far as calling him "Urs Hole" and printed his personal details. Things didn't stop there. Even once 16,000 abusive emails had been sent, reporters of the newspaper, *The Sun*, traveled to his hometown to place a giant England flag on a field near his home.

Even Polish Prime Ministers like to have a pop at referees. Following Howard Webb's decision to award Austria a penalty in Euro 2008 against Poland, Donald Tusk came out and said: "As the Prime Minister, I have to be balanced and collected. But on Thursday night, I was speaking very differently about the whole thing. I wanted to kill."

Perhaps the most bizarre case comes from Scotland. A linesman, Mike McCurry, disallowed an Aberdeen goal for offside in 2005. Ever since he has received a fine assortment of chicken giblets, razor blades and dead rats in his mailbox.

With this in mind, you can imagine how surreal it was to see A&M cornerback Deshazor Everett being ejected from the game for targeting. As Everett received his marching orders, I expected a furious volley of insults and vitriol to be directed at the officials. Instead, a chorus of light, unenergetic boos filled the air.

Luckily, I had learned from my previous experience of shouting expletives and remained calm. There was no need to create another scene. Or was there? Moments later, another big hit was slammed into a Rice receiver. This time I shouted a more polite phrase that once again gained the attention of my peers.

"CORR BLIMEY!"

The very second that these two ridiculously British words left my mouth, I suddenly realized how absurd this old-fashioned saying had sounded out loud. Compared to my foul-mouthed rant, I'd toned it down. What I hadn't foreseen were the roars of laughter that immediately surrounded me. In the plays that followed, numerous people joined in by shouting, "Corr Blimey!" at the top of their voices. Needless to say, my face was as maroon as the Aggies' uniforms. It may have been a bumpy ride, but my initiation was underway.

A particular aspect that stood out to me was the halftime entertainment. Back in Portsmouth, halftime is only useful for two things—going for a piss and grabbing a pie. Please note: it's not advisable to conduct these activities alongside each other.

In terms of entertainment, you're lucky if the work experience boy has the know-how to put the first half highlights on the stadium's decrepit, half-working big screen.

It hasn't always been so joyless, though. Back in the nineties, the club used to put on something exotic called the "dizzy stick." The rules were simple, but effective. There'd be two random blokes from the crowd that would be invited to take part. One ball was placed on the penalty spot in the middle of them. In order to get to the ball, kick it into the empty goal and win a £50 prize, these two (usually tipsy) competitors had to spin around a stick fifteen times.

Raucous mayhem always ensued. To the bellyaching laugher from the on-looking punters, the one that did it the quickest and got to the ball first always ended up stumbling to the floor in a bewildered and wobbly state.

It got to the point that if the soccer on display in the first half was awful, you'd turn around to the person behind and say, "Well, at least we've got the dizzy stick still to come!"

Unfortunately, due to health and safety reasons, and competitors regularly vomiting on the pitch, the concept soon came to an abrupt end. It was replaced with an inferior product, "Kick for a Car."

A local car company claimed if someone in the crowd could hit the crossbar from a hefty distance, they'd award them with a brand new set of wheels. At first it sounded like a nifty idea, even though we were still mourning the loss of our beloved dizzy stick.

Regrettably, the catch was that the company chose the competitors. Subsequently, they seemed to have a gift of plucking people that were so delirious they barely knew what day of the week it was. Laughably, this eventually came back to haunt them. Three months in, they picked someone that finally hit the crossbar and won the car. The next week we were informed the company had reneged on the offer, and had withdrawn all connections to the football club with immediate effect.

Since then, we've had nothing.

So, it was a lovely surprise when the following words roared through the scorching Texan heat:

"LADIES AND GENTLEMEN, NOW FORMING AT THE NORTH END OF KYLE FIELD, THE NATIONALLY FAMOUS FIGHTIN' TEXAS AGGIE BAND."

As 400 band members took their positions, I had no idea what to expect. Soon enough, I was transfixed with every move.

The choreography of the band almost didn't seem possible. I was breathless watching it, and not because I was effectively standing in a microwave. Just when I thought they had reached the crescendo, they would create another incredible formation that had me gasping with disbelief.

It must take hundreds of hours to perfect, and that's not even taking into consideration that they've got to do it in front of 90,000 onlookers. I was so impressed. It sounds cheesy, but it really did put the cherry on top of Kyle Field's unique and special atmosphere. On the subject of atmosphere, I was starting to digest the different yells that are recited during games. This was primarily due to a man in front of me bellowing them in an earsplitting fashion. The one that stuck out the most was:

Farmers fight!
Farmers fight!
Fight! Fight!
Farmers, farmers fight!

I stopped to reflect on the yells and songs that are belted out by the 12th Man. Whilst people slapped their biceps and yelled, "Beat the hell outta Rice!" I was again left perplexed. Other yells that reverberated around the stadium were:

Squads left! Squads right!
Farmers, farmers, we're all right!
Load, ready, aim, fire, BOOM!

A-G-G-I-E-S
A-G-G-I-E-S
Aaaaaaaa
Fight 'em, Aggies!

Rah! Rah! Rah! Rah!
T-A-M-C

Obviously, by this point in the day, I had already learned the hard way that colorful language is not acceptable in the world of college football. However, the yells were another glaring indication of how dissimilar the atmospheres of diverse sports can be. Everything I heard was a world away from the sort of stuff that is roared at soccer stadiums all over the United Kingdom.

To put this in context, here is a rundown of soccer songs that have been chanted on English terraces in recent years:

Manchester United celebrates the fact their South Korean midfielder, Park Ji-Sung, isn't from their rival city of Liverpool:

Park Park, wherever you may be,
You eat dogs in your home country,
But it could be worse, you could be Scouse,
Eating rats in your council house.

To the tune of "That's Amore" by Dean Martin—West Ham's song about their misfiring striker, Bobby Zamora:

When you're sat in row Z, and the ball hits your head, that's Zamora, that's Zamora.

A song about 6' 7" tall, beanpole striker, Peter Crouch:

He's big, he's red,
His feet stick out the bed,
Peter Crouch, Peter Crouch.

To the tune of the Adams family, Ipswich fans sing about their rivals, Norwich:

Your sister is your mother,
Your uncle is your brother,
*You all f*** one another,*
The Norwich family.

Liverpool striker Luis Suarez was found guilty of racially abusing an opposition player in 2011. The next week:

He cheats,
He dives,
He hates the Jackson Five,
Luis Suarez, Luis Suarez.

A timeless classic that's sung at any player, fan or official that is showing any sign of being remotely overweight:

Who ate all the pies? Who ate all the pies?
You fat bastard, you fat bastard, you ate all the pies!

Portsmouth fans celebrate the county that they reside in:

Oh South Hampshire,
Oh South Hampshire,
Is wonderful,
Is wonderful,
Oh South Hampshire is wonderful, its got tits, pussy and Pompey,
Oh South Hampshire is wonderful.

A Portsmouth song about "scummers"—a derogatory term for fans of Southampton FC:

He's only a poor little scummer,
His face is all tattered and torn,
He makes me feel sick,
So I hit him with a brick,
And now he don't sing anymore.

As you can tell, there are clearly some lyrical geniuses out there in the wrong day job. A predominant theme is to find a jingle and get it to rhyme. One that often stands out for me with its beautiful simplicity is a song about Zimbabwean striker, Benjani Mwaruwari:

Benjani, woah
Benjani, woah
He comes from Zimbabwe,
He's going to score today.

Literally, a four-year-old could come up with it. And yet, you find yourself shouting it as loudly as you can in sync with thousands of people for the duration of an afternoon.

Nine times out of ten, songs will be aimed at particular players, referees or the opposition's fans in the form of banter. Conversely, there have been numerous cases of where chants have crossed the ethical line. For instance, it is often reported that soccer fans sing unsympathetically about Manchester United's Munich air disaster in which 23 people died in 1958.

Furthermore, if you're a footballer and you're publically diagnosed with schizophrenia as Scottish goalkeeper Andy Goram was, the last thing you should expect is compassion. Rival supporters reveled in his diagnosis and chanted: "There's only two Andy Gorams!"

The stark contrast of Kyle Field to any English football stadium was mind-blowing. On the other hand, after hearing an Aggie yelling about farmers fighting, I was half expecting some good old-fashioned English football hooliganism to break out.

Instead, before the fourth quarter got underway, I soon reached the peak of my confusion. During my exploits of standing, sipping water and trying my best not to swear, I noticed the band had started to play at an increased volume. Everyone was joining in with a rhythmic tune I'd heard several times since arriving in Aggieland.

Without warning, something curious happened. A large, brutish man that had been sweating like a vegetarian in Fargo's BBQ, slung his damp arm around my neck.

Seconds later, we were swaying along with the rest of the stadium whilst singing, "Saw Varsity's horns off!"

It was like a dream seeing almost a hundred thousand people in unison, blasting out a chant that made little sense to me. I had a rough idea that the song was probably to do with the Texas Longhorns, but in fear of looking like a silly plank of wood, I decided to wait until I got back to my travel tavern to read up on the connotations of each yell.

Regardless, I found my jaw, yet again, on the floor. This was rapidly becoming a common theme. First midnight yell, second the marching band, and now some swaying extravaganza.

I adored every minute. It had reinforced my idea of entering Aggieland with basic, entry-level knowledge. Oh, and Texas A&M had just beaten the Owls 52-31 and to top things off, I was one of the rare few on my row that didn't pass out in the sweltering Texan sun.

11. Standing With The 12th Man

Once I'd strolled back to my travel tavern, I was feeling bloody brilliant basking in the glory of my fully air-conditioned room. As I ran a cold bath, I popped the TV on to catch some highlights of the victory over Rice. I was not prepared for what I was about to see. No, it wasn't footage of me attempting to saw Varsity's horns off.

ESPN analysts were passionately discussing Johnny Manziel. I presumed they'd be talking about his solid second-half performance in which he contributed three touchdown passes. I was wrong, very wrong. Instead, Johnny was getting it in the neck for earning a taunting penalty late in the fourth quarter.

Again, when it came to the reigning Heisman Trophy winner, everything had been blown out of proportion. It reminded me of the Manning Camp fiasco that had occurred earlier in the summer. Half of the media thought Johnny's decision to exit the camp after oversleeping wasn't the end of the world. The other half acted like he got drugged up to his eyeballs, taunted Peyton about having less Super Bowl rings than Eli, and finished off the evening by planting a right hook on their respected father, Archie.

On this Rice-related incident, one analyst claimed that as a result of the penalty, Jonny had lost the respect of his teammates. Moreover, he predicted A&M would crash and burn. I'd

113

never heard such rubbish in all of my life. He may as well have topped it off by labeling Manziel as the culprit behind the Israeli-Palestinian conflict.

At the time of the penalty, A&M was leading by 20-plus points. In the grand scheme of things, it didn't matter. And yet it was the only detail everyone wanted to preach about.

Following Johnny's epic entrance, you could tell the adrenaline was flowing. This was a unique occasion. Three days before he didn't know whether he'd ever wear the maroon and white again. When adrenaline flows you're prone to making poor judgment calls, which is admittedly what he did. Did he do anything that hadn't already been done by a dozen other players during the game? Nope. Yet the minute Johnny does it, the rules are different. He gets flagged and suddenly becomes the second coming of Adolf Hitler.

As soon as I'd stopped spitting feathers over this pointless debate, I looked up all of the different yells I'd heard earlier in the day. Four words stood out to me. "The Spirit of Aggieland." I had heard this phrase numerous times, and now realized it was the alma mater of the university. In addition, it refers to the "spirit can ne'er be told." This is the exceptional and unique school spirit that I'd already enjoyed a taste of.

Looking at the bigger picture, the whole idea of remaining impartial was already starting to wear thin. Figuratively speaking, the Kyle Field gameday experience had grabbed me by the knackers.

Throughout the game I felt the energy of my towel-waving increase with every play. Even though I had let myself down by expressing some deplorable language, I was beginning to absorb the required college football etiquette.

The weekdays seemed to fly by. It felt like I'd been in College Station barely five minutes, until I realized I'd been a guest in the State of Texas for over a week.

On reflection of my first seven days, I don't think I could have envisaged it going any better. When you can spend evenings in adventurous places such as Buffalo Wild Wings, you can have few complaints.

BWW is a place like no other. They have more television screens than I have ever seen in my lifetime. Anywhere there is space, there is a TV. I dread to think how much their electricity bill must be. Likewise, on the night I first attended they were buying into one of England's proudest traditions—the pub quiz. In a sea of booze and chicken, I was wonderfully informed that Cuba is 777 miles long.

Talking of great places to go, earlier in the week I discovered one of the most bizarre concepts I'd ever seen. Harvey Washbangers. Here you can drink beer, eat burgers and do your laundry. Yep, that's right, do your laundry. So, if you ever fancy munching on a cheeseburger, swigging a craft beer—all while your whites and smalls frantically spin in front of you (and let's face it, who wouldn't?), then you're in luck.

I'm afraid to say it hadn't all been cookies and cream in my escapades around the Brazos Valley. I had an episode of light embarrassment during my time at BJ's Restaurant & Brewhouse near Post Oak Mall on Labor Day. Whilst tucking into a mountain of spaghetti and meat sauce, a song from my favorite band, Oasis, embraced the airwaves. A huge sense of English nostalgia filled me up, and naturally I began to mime the lyrics to myself. In hindsight, it wasn't a good call.

By the time the second chorus circled around, I was deep in discussion with an on-looking stranger who'd noticed I was enjoying the soothing tones of the Gallagher brothers. The gentleman enquired if I originated from Australia. Funnily enough, this was the third time such a presumption had been made. When I informed him that I was actually from the United Kingdom, he seemed disappointed.

Language was still something I struggled to get to grips with. Shock horror, we both speak English. However, the slang used by Brits and Yanks could not be more different. I was trying hard to Americanize a lot of my words just so I didn't receive baffled looks in return. Luckily, you soon get used to it. I quickly learned the phrases and idioms that caused the most chaos. For example, I was really cutting down on using the word "mate." I can't help myself. At home everyone uses it. In the US, it has no currency. This comes with audible complications. As a replacement, saying the word "dude" or "buddy" in a British accent sounds plain wrong.

Eventually, a scenario on a Sunday night perfectly outlined the cultural barrier. During the process of destroying a large pepperoni pizza in an elegant establishment known as Double Daves, I realized that NFL Sunday Night Football was broadcasting on an alternative channel to the one we were being treated to. I waltzed over to the counter and politely asked if they could replace whatever Kardashian product was on for the glorious sights of Carrie Underwood. Pandemonium ensued. A man, who I presumed was the manager, came out to see what unrest was waiting for him.

"Can I help you, sir?" he nervously probed.

"Yeah, please can you put football on?"

He looked mystified as he shuffled through the EPG.

"Umm, I don't think we get the soccer channels."

"Ohhh. No, I want football. Your football! Sunday Night Football has gotten underway. I think it's on NBC."

For some unknown reason, he couldn't quite get his head around what I was asking for. Was I speaking in fluent Korean? A fellow employee even came out to see if he could help find the channel. Despite seeing NBC and the words, "NFL SUNDAY NIGHT FOOTBALL" show up on the guide multiple times, I let it slide. By that point I'd almost completed my pepperoni assault course. The whole episode seemed farcical. How many Double Daves' employees does it take to change a channel? I guess I'll never know. In fairness, their pizza is so damn good I wasn't that bothered in the end.

Alongside language and basic misunderstood requests, other cultural differences emerged. For one, it had seeped in that walking was an unacceptable form of transport around these parts. On three consecutive days people in cars slammed their brakes, wheeled their windows down and shouted generic insults, such as, "Walking sucks!" "Hey! Walking is for losers, man!" and my personal favorite, "Get a car, you jackass!"

Unfortunately, as they sped away into the distance, I didn't get to inform them off my modest budget or tell the rather large fellow that called me a jackass that perhaps some walking would do him good once in a while. Truthfully, it didn't bother me at all. As far as I was concerned, even though walking in soaring temperatures had a serious downside, it was making me feel far less guilty about all the wonderful food and drink that I was consuming.

I'd always considered America to be the UK's cool, big brother. This was backed up by a series of subtle nuances I'd uncovered. The first one might seem puzzling, but in my mind it's pure genius. Back in England, when you're watching soccer at a pub or bar and you need to go to the toilet, without fail you always seem to miss either a goal or something important. How have the people of America got around this conundrum? Stick a TV in the toilets! Simple and effective. Although it doesn't exactly help your aim.

On the eccentric topic of lavatories, why does America insist on calling them bathrooms and restrooms? Has anyone gone for a leak and noticed someone casually sitting inside a bathtub? Or chatted to a fellow human and they've said, "I'm good. Just having a bit of a rest. It's been a long day and I'm utterly exhausted."

On the other hand, a cultural upgrade I enjoyed is when your wallet is full of $1 bills. In England, the smallest currency you can get in note-form is £5. So when you're promenading around Texas and have that "full wallet feeling" when in reality you've only got $8 to your name, it can be tremendously fulfilling.

With such an illustrious amount of cash burning a hole in my pocket, I couldn't help but stop by at the local supermarket. It was a monstrous structure with the letters "H-E-B" emblazoned across the top. I'd describe my first visit as memorable. The first thing I refused to believe was how empty it was. My local supermarket in Guildford is like a battlefield. Without fail you will see trolleys crashing into the meat aisle, children using pineapples as weapons, and on a somber day the final loaf of bread will not cause a fatality.

In HEB, it was like there'd been an apocalypse and I'd turned up to loot for supplies. Even though there was a lack of customers, there certainly wasn't a shortage of employees. I required three different store managers to verify that a British passport is an accepted form of identification. The third supervisor who eventually gave me the green light even had the cheek to flick through my passport, look at the stamps and ask how each place was. It was audacious, but I was so impressed they pack your groceries for you that I humored him and went on my merry way.

Whilst carrying my rustic brown bag full of HEB's own brand salted chips and a case of Sam Adams, I pondered the possible reasons behind why the supermarket had been so deserted. Was it because they interrogate everyone about their travel history? The answer quickly dawned on me. It's because eating out is so damn good. Why cook when you can eat out? It's less effort, more social and in some places, cheaper. Plus the service you get is first class. This was something I wasn't accustomed to at home. There is a tipping culture in the US that doesn't exist in England. Instead, we get mopey and depressed waiters standing around staring at the clock and counting down the seconds until their shift ends. Because they get a fixed wage, they have no motivation to go the extra mile.

Mathematics isn't my strong point. Luckily, I'd managed to tip effectively everywhere I'd been. Well, when I say that, it meant I hadn't had any waiters or bartenders chasing me down the street.

Food seemed more authentic. With so much competition around, your grub has to be either really good or really cheap. Everyone is a winner.

Well, except my waistline.

On the Friday before Texas A&M's second game of the season against Sam Houston State, I made my Northgate debut.

If you don't know, Northgate is the place where the students of Texas A&M hang out. Located a stone's throw away from campus, it's a strip of bars, bars and more bars. Oh, and the odd chicken shop. Essentially, it is a place that if I were still a student, I would probably never leave. And by the looks of it, many people don't. It's pretty much busy all day long.

Anyway, I had visited as I'd been invited along to watch the USA men's soccer team take on Costa Rica in an important World Cup qualifier. I was more than happy to get behind "The Stars and Stripes," and hopefully cheer them to victory.

After the opening ten minutes, that was looking increasingly unlikely; they were already 2-0 down. I presumed I was a jinx, especially as they had won their last twelve games in a row. They ended up losing the game 3-1. Sorry, chaps.

Across the pond we have our own version of student nightlife. This could not be more different. In the UK, if you visited any town after 9:00 p.m. you'd be treated to a skyline of anarchy. Police swarm the streets as fighting and anti-social behavior breaks out in every direction. Our legal drinking age is 18, so that certainly contributes to the mayhem. Not that I'd want to wait until I'm 21 to start drinking, though. Not that many people in Northgate do. I was there for a solitary night and could tell an under-age drinker a mile off. Let's just say it's certainly handy if you've got a friend that's over 21, or you know a shady individual that can produce a legitimate Hawaiian, McLovin-esque ID.

Everything seemed more civil. People were out for a genuinely good time. Nevertheless, I must admit I was growing a little nostalgic for witnessing a brutal English punch-up in the street.

I did see some things that surprised me. When I first arrived, sixty people dressed in what I can only describe as "cowboy gear" walked straight past me. At that point I hadn't had a cold beverage yet, although it felt like I was tripping.

Please bear in mind I'd never seen a cowboy in real life before—let alone sixty in one serving.

Whilst visiting the Dixie Chicken, or The Chicken as it's affectionately known, I was completely in awe. This was Texas. This was a place that typified how this state is portrayed in films and TV shows all around the world. It was like a set from a spaghetti western movie. From the wooden swinging doors to people playing dominoes on the tables, it was brilliant. My imagination ran wild. I expected Clint Eastwood to pop around the corner at any moment. Unfortunately, he did not. Maybe next time?

Do you know what's worse than a standard hangover? A hangover in excruciatingly high temperatures.

I'd only experienced this type of brain-splitting headache once or twice on vacation before. It hit me like a ton of bricks. Usually to alleviate the pain, I'd find myself chomping down a full English breakfast. Where in College Station could I find a suitable substitute? Oh yes, my trusty ally. Denny's.

The journey there was insufferable. My legs felt like jelly as the Texan sun pierced and stabbed its way through my forehead. In every sense of the word, I was struggling. Moreover, I was seemingly oblivious to my surroundings as I walked past a group of students running around with broomsticks tucked between their legs. Instead of querying why this curious gang were playing Quidditch in a nearby field, my eye was firmly on the prize: a big plate of meat, eggs and toast.

With alcohol continuing to seep through my every pore, there she was—the wonderful red and yellow sign. It may as well have read "HEAVEN."

121

Once I'd entered and mopped my brow, I was devastated to find a thirty-minute wait for a table. I slumped into a nearby chair as I mournfully watched copious amounts of food delivered to lucky recipients.

Finally, it was my time to shine. My tragic table for one had been prepared.

"One Lumberjack Slam, please," I gleefully requested.

"Hash browns or grits?" asked the waitress.

Wait. When I previously ordered the exact same meal, this question wasn't part of the dialogue. I became flustered. I had no idea what grits were. Regardless, I had to man up and make a judgment call. She looked nervous as I prepared to make my announcement.

"Grits, please."

A voice in my head screamed "WHAT!? You love a hash brown. Grits sound gruesome! What on earth are you playing at?"

This voice had a valid point. However, I was feeling adventurous.

Fast-forward twenty minutes and I was heavily regretting my decision. Even though a portion of these so-called grits lay in front of me, I neither knew, nor wanted to know, what they were.

Once I was finished, the waitress came to collect my plate. She saw through my childish trick of spreading a bit here and there to make it look like I had some.

"Should have gone for the hash browns, huh?" she joked.

I vowed to never make such a schoolboy error again.

With a later kickoff time of 6:00 p.m. penciled in, I was relieved that I wouldn't have to experience the sweltering mid-day temperatures of the week before. Furthermore, I had learned you could take your own water into the stadium—no more paying $5 per bottle for me.

I can openly admit to being a superstitious sports fan. When I attend Portsmouth matches and they are victorious, I will make sure I wear the exact same jersey for the next game. Oh, and if I'm feeling like we need an extra dose of luck, there's a good chance I'll wear the same underwear, too.

Over the years, this has developed into an almost psychotic feature of mine. It's stretched from jerseys to entering the stadium through my lucky turnstile. As much as the hangover contributed to my Denny's visit, the superstitious routine demanded it.

The grits debacle had put me out of sync. Luckily, I was too hungover to waste another second worrying about it. Fortunately, by mid-afternoon I was starting to perk up a bit. The big breakfast had paid off. It was now time to make my way to the stadium.

I was due to meet a student called Kyle at the twelfth man statue shortly before kickoff. Whilst waiting for him to show up, I couldn't help but be impressed by the statue's presence and meaning. The twelfth man tradition dates back to 1922. During a game against Centre College, the Aggies had suffered many injuries and were down to their last eleven players. Their coach, Dana X. Bible, recalled a squad member that wasn't suited or in pads. He was with the press, helping them to identify players. Soon enough, he was called from the stands and asked to stand ready until the game finished. He was quite literally the twelfth man.

Nowadays, the complete student body is referred to as the twelfth man. They stand throughout the whole game in a bid to show their support and that if called upon, they are ready. Also, a little gem I discovered was that one member of the Aggies kickoff team is a regular student. How cool would that be?

Well, not as cool as watching someone eat six consecutive packets of Doritos. I was mesmerized as I watched this man consume bag after bag of the popular corn-based snack. He even still had room to devour half a toffee apple. I almost felt a duty to go and shake this man's hand for his truly remarkable achievement. Before I had the opportunity, Kyle appeared.

Within minutes we were through the turnstiles and about to embark on a few glorious hours of Aggie football. This experience would be much different compared to last week. I wasn't going to be surrounded by the general admission lot. Instead, I had joined the beating heart and soul of the university—the students.

A week prior, I had sat opposite them. My jaw regularly dropped to the floor as different yells and gestures were carried out in unison by a wall of 30,000 people.

This time, I was in the thick of the largest student section in the country. Following Kyle's generous offer to sneak me in, I wasn't about to turn down the opportunity to join a mob that were thirsty for Sam Houston State's blood—not literally, may I add—I hadn't had the pleasure of meeting any vampires in the Lone Star State, and doubted I ever would. Never say never, though.

I will admit my knowledge of SHSU was minimal at best. Funnily enough, I didn't know that Sam Houston was actually Texas' version of George Washington until long after the game. As a substitute, I was under the impression that it may have just been a suburb of Houston. With this in mind, to bring the hate upon them felt a little wrong, but hell to it, with English football hooliganism in my ancestry, I was ready to roll. Until the rain came.

Since landing in Houston, I had barely seen a cloud, let alone a drop of the wet stuff. It was sod's law that the first time the heavens opened during my stay was as the game kicked off. With thunder and lightning growling in the distance, the game quickly took its course. Johnny Manziel was racking up yardage all over the place. He exited in the third quarter with 426 passing yards under his belt.

Both rushing and receiving opportunities were shared across the board. In total, eleven receivers got a chance to show Coach Sumlin what they were made of. In particular, it was a coming out party for senior wide receiver, Travis Labhart. After being a part of the Aggie football program for the two previous years, he was finally handed a stage to perform on. He didn't disappoint and went onto become an integral part of A&M's 2013 offense. Another receiver that stood out was LaQuvionte Gonzalez. I could safely say that I'd never come across a name as outlandish as LaQuvionte in my time around the British highlands.

With 93 total points tiring the busy individual that updates the scoreboard, Kyle Field had forgotten about the weather and was rocking. Before the game, not many people had given SHSU a sniff. If truth be told, they had to be applauded for racking up 28 points. At least it gave the small pockets of orange around Kyle Field something to cheer about. Unfortunately folks, your mascot still looks like an evil version of the Frosted Flakes figurehead, Tony the Tiger.

So, what did I make of the student section? Well, I now appreciated why there weren't many overweight students occupying the bleachers of the east side of Kyle Field. With all the yells, it's simply exhausting. The amount of exercise you undertake throughout a game is probably equivalent to an extended gym session. I was gasping for breath at points.

Overall, it's certainly different to sitting with the general admissions. Every few minutes the yell leaders start doing what I can only describe as an enthusiastic jig, and consequently the students know what's coming. To begin with, I won't lie; I was like a fish out of water. Everyone around me knew exactly what to do. Me? I just copied everyone else, but was two seconds behind. In fact, if you gave me the option to watch myself back, I genuinely don't think I could do it. The embarrassment would be too much for me.

I was determined to get there. By the time the game was coming to a close, I had learned a majority of the different nuances. For example, as the field goal kicker, Taylor Bertolet, goes up to strike the ball, the Aggies hold up crossed fingers and start praying for a good outcome. Apparently, this was because Mr. Bertolet had a reputation for being an erratic kicker. Furthermore, an integral symbol of Aggieland is giving a thumbs-up. As the opposing team's punter kicks the ball to A&M, every member of the student section raises and shakes their thumbs. It's an odd and baffling concept written down, and like many things around Aggieland—it only makes sense when you see it in action.

And within that last paragraph is a subject in itself. The perception and reality of Texas A&M, and what makes the place so special. Various people describe it as having a unique school spirit that "from the outside looking in, you can't understand it. And from the inside looking out, you can't explain it."

That quote could not be more fitting. If I had been teleported to this game and had no previous understanding of the history or traditions, I'd believe this society was borderline strange, especially once I was told a mysterious man that went by the name "Visor Guy" was effectively a sixth yell leader.

Similarly, there were other aspects I struggled to get my head around. One that stood out the most was a group of cadets standing by the field with swords tucked at their waists. Swords? At a sporting event? Health and safety sirens sounded, along with a memory that dated back to 1998. Sheffield United had traveled down to Portsmouth for a league game. Ironically, Sheffield's nickname is "The Blades." Why the irony? Well, halfway through the first half one of their nutcase fans stormed the field and stabbed a linesman before fleeing the scene. Perhaps if Portsmouth employed these park rangers with swords swinging in rhythm with their hips, such incidents might be prevented.

In no uncertain terms, from an outside view looking in, Texas A&M seemed peculiar. However, even in my short time in College Station, I was beginning to no longer consider myself as an outsider. The more I spoke to people, developed friendships and got to grips with the core values of Aggieland, every single intricacy started to make perfect sense.

Now, I could tell my currently non-existent grandchildren that I had stood on the front line with the 12th Man. That alone topped off a great day in which the Aggies stormed to a 65-28 victory. The wheels were firmly in motion for the next seven days.

The bammers were coming to town.

12. 'BAMA WEEK

When you're growing up, September is considered to be the worst month of all. Why? Because after the long, beautiful and warm summer holidays, you are summoned back to reality. The memories of playing Rollercoaster Tycoon and The Sims until four o'clock in the morning are long gone.

Instead, you find yourself doing homework and wishing your life away as you quietly pray that next summer comes around in a flash. Amongst this melee of depressed students and school children is a breed of people that live for this underrated 30-day cycle.

Football fans. Oh yes. This is the time of year when your weekend schedule begins to be consumed by one activity—sitting on your arse, drinking multiple beers and cheering your team to glory. Starting with ESPN's College GameDay on Saturday morning and ending with NFL's Sunday Night Football, your weekends are officially sorted until February.

This rigorous timetable requires dedication. It's harder than it sounds watching football non-stop. Unfortunately, real life does not understand the importance and rituals that go hand-in-hand with the lifestyle of a diehard football fan.

As a result, you quickly find yourself acting in an abnormal and suspicious fashion. For example, as soon as your partner asks you to visit the supermarket during a juicy SEC showdown, you've got to be alert and ready to brandish a believable excuse. Failure to do so can result in your television being thrown out of the nearest window.

Likewise, it is your responsibility to arrange compulsory events around football games of less importance. I know what you're thinking: every game is important! This is true. However, when push comes to shove, sacrifices such as missing the New York Jets vs. Jacksonville Jaguars have to be tactically played. Furthermore, it's advised you make it obvious to your spouse or significant other that you've foregone something wonderful (even though it's not, sorry Jets and Jags) for a mind-numbingly boring, six-year-old's birthday party.

It is also recommended you adhere to a decent training and fitness regime in the weeks and months leading up to this glorious section of the calendar. This is imperative, because the only exercise you will get from September onwards is the short walk to the fridge and back as you fetch another beer. Thanks to modern technology and the invention of the portable mini-fridge, even this small excursion is slowly dying out.

With the man cave in full flow, you're in your element. Nothing can get you down. Well, that's not entirely true. You are always at the mercy of outside influences, such as the moment your partner announces: "Bob and Marie have invited us to go fishing on Saturday afternoon. I think it would be wonderful. What do you think?"

Horror saturates your face as you quickly explore the archives to muster up a tangible excuse. Puzzlement. Screw Bob. You've never liked him. Why socialize with someone that organizes exploits during football season? That's not someone you should be associated with. Plus, Marie talks about her kids way too much.

You are on your own. There's nowhere to hide; you have to give in and take one for the team. Or do you? Your destiny is always in your own hands. It's time to put Plan B into action.

The night before the dreaded fishing trip, subtly complain about a dodgy stomach. Following a quick trip to the bathroom in which you've lightly covered your face with a sprinkling of mild water, waltz back and say your temperature is a cause for concern. Rule one—commence slowly. Too much too early will give the game away. Do not over egg the pudding.

After leaving it an hour or so, it's time to increase the volume and become visibly upset that it's purely your luck to get sick after a long, hard week at work. Play the sympathy card.

Before bed, take longer in the bathroom than usual. Much longer. Turn the usual routine on its head. Tip: take your phone in with you to help pass the time. Once your partner senses something is awry and asks if you are OK, brush it off and stay cool. Any big plays at this stage could still result in separation or divorce.

Throughout the night, visit the toilet at regular intervals. It is essential you do this as loudly as possible. No, I don't mean start smashing pots and pans with a wooden spoon, but create precisely enough noise to make your partner realize that you're jogging to the thunderbox in the middle of the night.

In the wake of a seemingly rough evening in which you've reached a socially acceptable level on Angry Birds, it's time to release the Kraken.

"Darling, you know I've been excited for this fishing trip... but my stomach was doing summersaults last night. I was in agony at one point. I must have eaten something..." Before you get a reaction, deliver the killer blow.

"I don't know what restroom facilities the boat has, but I'm definitely going to need a toilet close by. I'm not sure I can hold on for a whole afternoon. I suppose if things escalate, I could take a dump hanging off the edge of the boat. Do you think Bob and Marie would be OK with that?"

And with that solitary image burned into the eyeballs of your partner, you have just bought yourself a day pass for one on the couch.

In another visit to the infamous Buffalo Wild Wings hideout, I observed the Houston Texans take on the San Diego Chargers. Within the first five minutes I had witnessed some rare scenes.

The minute San Diego scored a touchdown, a flip-flop, yes, a flip-flop, was flung at the projector showing the game. I could safely say I'd never seen that before. A part of me longed for more touchdowns solely to see what else would be chucked. I soon realized that I was seated uncomfortably close to the screen.

Inside my danger zone, I comforted myself with a bevy of cheeseburger slammers. These bundles of ecstasy were surrounded by their own valley of fries. I hadn't seen a salad in weeks. It comes to something when you begin to view anything that's not accompanied by fries as a healthy and nutritious meal.

On the subject of things I hadn't seen yet, I'd been lucky enough to not bump into one of the characteristics that Texas is most famous for—guns. Then again, there was a period of time when I would have quite happily come across a rifle and blown my feet off. Oh the blisters. Walking ten miles a day in 100-degree heat had taken its toll. Back in England, I used to barely know what walking was. Now, my lower body was in ruins. As well as shin splints, I had blisters that were the size of conservatory light bulbs. At times I was in unrivaled distress and heavily considered getting a pair of rootin' tootin' cowboy boots. After all, everyone else wore them; they had to be comfortable, right?

Before I dwelled on the sorry state of my crippled legs any longer, I began to address my immediate future. Next weekend the back-to-back National Champions, Alabama, were coming to town. So far I hadn't had any luck with sourcing somewhere to stay for Friday or Saturday. In addition, my attempts to try and get a ticket for the game had fallen flat on their face.

On the Monday morning it dawned on me that time was promptly running out on both fronts. The thought of missing one of 2013's biggest college football games and spending two nights on the street didn't exactly have me jumping for joy.

After calling every single hotel and motel in the Bryan and College Station area, I started to panic. Everywhere was full to the brim. My mind drifted. Should I simply go to Houston for the weekend? At least there I'd have a comfortable bed and be able to watch the game on TV. As Monday progressed, this option was becoming more viable with every minute that went by. I did feel safe in Aggieland, and predicted I could easily get away with one night, but two? With all my belongings, that'd be a big ask. The more I thought about it, the crazier it seemed.

Whilst warming to the Houston idea, my mind quickly backtracked. I'd come to Texas for these types of occasions, and the last thing I should be doing is running away from them.

That's when it hit me. During my first midnight yell I'd joked to Jeff, who worked for the University Police Department, that I had nowhere to stay for the Alabama weekend. At that point I was hopeful I'd be able to source somewhere in the weeks that followed.

Anyone who knows Jeff will know what his response was to my admittance. Even though I was effectively a complete stranger and had only known him for a grand total of ten minutes, he offered me a place to stay. It's people like Jeff that typified why I was falling in love with Texas. Here I was, completely out of my depth, a long way from home, and through a coincidence of going to Kyle Field at that particular time, met someone that would be like a big brother throughout my stay.

In the days leading up to the weekend, I saw Jeff and nervously floated the idea of me crashing at his place for a couple of nights. My heart was firmly in my mouth as I approached the subject. Jeff was his typical self, good as gold and said he'd love to have me over. To this day I still can't thank him enough. Because of his unbelievably generous hospitality, I could now focus on my next task.

Since arriving on Texan soil, I had been on the search for one thing—a golden ticket. With September 14th drawing closer and closer, my chances of getting one were dwindling.

I had acquired tickets to the other games through the 12th Man Foundation, but an Alabama ticket was one I had no guarantee of getting because the demand was sky high. For example, in the lead up to the game, *Forbes Magazine* had reported that the A&M-Alabama game was projected to be one of the most expensive and sought after sporting tickets of all time. Gulp.

Twenty-four hours before the heavyweight bout, tickets on Stubhub were averaging at $863 each.

However, I hadn't traveled five thousand miles to miss one of the biggest sporting events in Texas A&M history, and a once-in-a-lifetime opportunity. As soon as my plane landed in Houston, I tried to get peace of mind by getting a ticket to the game as early as possible.

I asked dozens of people if they knew someone with a spare. That question was always met with laughs and the same old response: "No. Good luck with finding one."

Sporadically, you would get the odd character that'd say their best friend's fiancée's new dog might have one. I was at rock bottom.

All was not lost. With five days to go until kickoff, the ticket God's looked down favorably upon me. I had a message that suggested there might be some much needed light at the end of the tunnel. I was put in touch with someone who was 60-70% sure they had a ticket available. More importantly, it wouldn't cost me a wallet-shattering price of $800. The drawback was I'd have to wait a grueling 48 hours to find out if the ticket was up for grabs. Being brutally honest, I had no other options—I was happy to be patient and hope for the best.

The 48 hours passed. Not a sausage. I began to worry, and cursed myself for wasting two days when I could have been exploring other avenues. I was close to giving up, and had already chosen to watch the game at Sully's Sports Grill & Bar.

On that Thursday, the chap that said he may have a ticket got in touch. It was good news. We quickly arranged to meet by the trolleys in a HEB parking lot. Not the classiest of places for such a transaction, but I wasn't complaining. As long as he had the ticket, it could have been in the middle of the Gaza Strip for all I cared.

At our rendezvous, all I knew was that he was going to be wearing a black t-shirt. I had got to the supermarket at the agreed time and waited with bated breath.

A few minutes went by. There was no sign of this mysterious ticket-selling entrepreneur. I got twitchy. Finally, I clocked a black t-shirted man and hesitantly greeted him. He passed me the ticket and my legs wobbled with joy. I handed over $400. If any police were about, they would have suspected us for dealing drugs. But no, the only thing we were dealing was sporting euphoria.

With my accommodation and ticket to the big game sorted, I was now in a position to enjoy the craziness of 'Bama week. In a whirlwind of outrageous ticket prices, ESPN/CBS rocking up with 700 lorries each, and rumors of rapper and songwriter Drake making an appearance, the week was beginning to live up to the expected hype.

The only people that didn't know Alabama was taking on Texas A&M on Saturday either lived under a rock or had recently woken up from a coma.

As much as I was looking forward to the game, a big part of me wished I could bottle up the anticipation and excitement that surrounded the Brazos Valley. The news there were plans to bring out a *Jurassic Park 4* movie and a TV series focusing on *Breaking Bad's* criminal lawyer Saul Goodman, had been the icing on the cake.

Everyone sensed we were on the brink of a very special occasion. For Alabama, the game was all about one component—revenge. A&M was the only team that beat them in 2012. As you can imagine, Johnny Manziel making such a prestigious team look silly in their own backyard did not go down well with the locals. Subsequently, they had resorted to low blows, such as making mockery piñatas of the Aggies' quarterback.

Moreover, there was speculation that pockets of the 10,000 'Bama fans expected in town had a couple of pranks up their sleeves. Earlier in the week one brave soul had already draped the Alabama logo over the "Welcome to Texas A&M University" sign. My advice: take the Corps of Cadets on at your peril.

After paying such a heavy chunk of coin for a ticket, I was desperate for the two sides to deliver. Just the thought of the celebrations in Northgate made victory so mouth-watering, let alone the National Championship implications.

Furthermore, I'd already decided that if Deshazor Everett made another match-winning interception against the Crimson Tide, my first child would be named in honor of him, regardless if it were a boy or a girl.

With the fresh visions of an oblivious son or daughter of mine bumbling around the English counties with the name Deshazor, I was equally reveling in the atmosphere around Aggieland. No other words were spoken other than discussion about the pending game.

There were so many unknown variables. How would A&M's defense do with their key players returning? What did

Nick Saban have up his sleeve for Johnny? What impact was the 12th Man going to have? The list went on and on. And that's why everything that surrounded the game was as exciting as the time a stray dog appeared at my school in 1995. No one could predict what was going to happen. A&M could destroy Alabama. Alabama could destroy A&M. One point could win it. There were endless eventualities.

The night before the game, for one more night, the Aggies continued to dream. Five years before, I made the trip to Wembley Stadium, London. My beloved soccer team, Portsmouth, had reached their first FA Cup Final in 69 years. Like A&M, my team had suffered decades of failing to reach their potential. We were cast aside in the soccer world for so long. In 2008, it was our time. During the final with the scores tied at 0-0, I prayed to the skies and whispered: "Please, please, let us win. I don't care if we lose every game for the next five years. I want this cup so badly!"

Whoever answered that call took it literally. Portsmouth went on to win the trophy, but since have been relegated countless times and now sit at the very bottom of England's professional football pyramid.

Was this going to be A&M's time? In less than 24 hours, we'd find out. The night before the game a music concert was put on at Kyle Field. It featured local artists such as Lyle Lovett, Robert Earl Keen, Emmylou Harris and Rodney Crowell.

I'm not going to pretend that I'd heard of any of them, but with the euphoria and apprehension around town I thought the atmosphere alone would be worth sampling.

For the first time in my life, I experienced country music. My prior knowledge of this music genre was shockingly bad. Embarrassingly, the only country singers I knew were Taylor Swift (always in the UK newspapers) and John Rich (saw him on *The Celebrity Apprentice*). I was scared this lack of knowledge could land me in hot water with the locals.

Once I'd turned up at Kyle Field, I made my way to the section printed on my ticket. I'd go as far as saying that I probably ended up with the worst seat in the house. As well as barely being able to see the stage, the acoustics didn't travel well in the slightest. The people around me were equally fed up, and longed for somewhere you could actually examine what was going on. Usually, I'd be far too scared to speak up and complain, but even I sensed how pointless the next couple of hours would be if we remained where we were.

I went over to one of the supervisors and asked if they could move us to a better location. It was clear that the concert hadn't sold out. The supervisor apologized and said it was out of his hands.

By this point, a Friday night in Northgate was becoming increasingly appetizing. With midnight yell a few hours away, I made a snap decision to go and enjoy a few cold beverages in Northgate and return to Kyle Field for the main event.

As I walked down the ramp I noticed a handful of people were still arriving. With this in mind, I wondered if it was going to be a problem that I wanted to leave. Surely not? They can't try and make me stay, can they?

The second the words "Hi, can you let me out please?" left my mouth, it was as if I'd notified them that I had a bomb strapped to my vest.

Silence. The blatant disbelief on the face of the steward was evident.

"No. You are not allowed out. There are strictly no readmissions."

I paused. I could tell this was going to be trickier than I initially imagined.

"Yes, I know; I don't mind. You won't have to readmit me. I want to go and get something to eat."

"Food and beverages are available at the concession stands."

It was clear that he wasn't getting the message. It was time to turn it up a notch.

"Yes, I know. But I also need to meet a friend."

"Tickets are still available," he said sarcastically.

It was like pulling teeth. For some unknown reason, he couldn't get his head around the notion that I wanted to depart the premises. Hail Mary time.

"Tickets? What? No. There's been an emergency. I need to leave now."

"Hungry? A friend? Now an emergency...."

Before he had time to say anything else, I interjected.

"JUST LET ME LEAVE!"

And with those four crushing words echoing through the cool evening air, I noticed someone on the other side of the turnstile looking back at me. Horrified. It was Texas A&M University President, Richard Bowen Loftin.

Finally, I was allowed out. As I slumped off into the night, the thought that President Loftin may banish me from A&M began to resonate. Fortunately, I'd soon be lifted by the soothing sight of Northgate in the distance.

Off the back of four pints of Shiner Bock and a plate of chicken, I was on the move again. The walk to midnight yell was always a stroll I looked forward to. As you inch closer to the bright and dazzling lights of Kyle Field, you can sense and feel the atmosphere building. This midnight yell practice was projected to be slightly different. There had been predictions that as many as 50,000 people could turn out.

After meeting Jeff at his usual gate, it was becoming increasingly apparent that we were in for a truly special event. With ESPN screening it live, the Aggies put on a show. It was officially the most attended midnight yell in Texas A&M history. My only gripe was that it was over in a flash. I could've happily sung "Spirit of Aggieland" and the "Aggie War Hymn" on repeat for several hours.

With droves of people exiting the stadium, everyone was on the same wavelength. Hurry up 2:30 p.m. tomorrow. I was thinking the same, but with the added motive—I hope I don't bump into President Loftin on my way out.

On the morning of the game, College Station had a definitive and profound atmosphere. Compared to the Rice and Sam Houston State games, you could tell this one really mattered.

I headed to Kyle Field early to soak up the environment and experience ESPN's College GameDay that was being filmed on campus.

Five minutes into my journey, I was struggling with the heat. I felt the same way as I did the very first time I strolled down South Texas Avenue. I don't know if it was a cocktail of nerves, excitement or the blistering sun that was getting to me. What I did know is if I didn't stop and take in some liquids, I'd soon pass out on the side of the road.

Water had never tasted so good. As it sloshed through my frame, I immediately felt some energy in my legs again. Following this brief hiccup, it was time to continue my trek past the golf course and into the shadows of the stadium.

Once I arrived, I had guessed the GameDay set would be easy to find. It wasn't. In my first few weeks at A&M, the campus confused the hell out of me. Every time I ambled around the concourses, I'd soon get lost. Kyle Field was always my get out of jail free card. I'd simply look for the monstrous structure and work out where I was accordingly.

With time on my hands, I checked out the tailgating scene. I was astonished. Even at 10:00 a.m. people were knocking back shots of tequila. Equally as impressive, these tailgates seemed to stretch as far as the eye could see. Literally thousands of people surrounded Kyle Field as they ate and drank to their hearts' content. Back home, this would never happen. As well as it being far too cold, miserable and wet to socialize in the open, people often congregate in nearby drinking grounds such as pubs and bars.

Whilst standing in this mighty assembly of people, something caught my eye. It was a man eating an entire cucumber. He chomped down the whole thing, skin included. I feared that I was suffering from heat stroke and was beginning to experience hallucinations.

Shortly after this jaunt, I plucked up the courage to ask a group of tailgaters if they knew where College GameDay was being filmed. In reply, a dude drunkenly threw his arms at a building and gestured it'd be somewhere in that general area. Luckily, it was. Cheers bro.

Unfortunately, I soon realized GameDay isn't actually that fun if you're standing a hundred yards away from the action and not waving a ten-foot sign around like a madman. I moved on.

By this time it was getting closer and closer to kickoff. I clenched onto my ticket like it was gold dust. Naturally, I fear the worst. So, you can imagine my anxiety when I noticed everyone else's ticket looked considerably different to mine. After shelling out an extortionate amount of change for it, the thought I'd been scammed started to set in. I longed for the gates to open so I could find out. The wait was severe.

As I got in line, I positioned myself into the ironically named "Express Lane." I had visions of us all powering through in an efficient manner. Instead, I was subjected to a bout of torment. A husband and wife had lost one of their tickets and refused to go to the back of the queue until the flustered lady eventually found it in the depths of her inappropriately large handbag.

People had been shouting at them to hurry up. Had I? Of course not. English people are built to queue without showing any signs of discontent. On average, I predict Brits spend at least ten years of their lifespan in a queue. It's just something we do, and we do it well.

Finally, once I'd showcased my queuing expertise, I handed my ticket over. The green light came up on the scanner. Joy. Delight. Rapture. I was in. Regrettably, others weren't so lucky. Later that day I heard some horror stories on the subject of fake tickets. One case really stuck in my head. Two couples were queuing to get into the stadium and striked up a jovial conversation. Naturally, one of them asked where the other was sitting. Once they compared where they were located, they realized both pairs of tickets were exact duplicates. They'd been scammed into spending hundreds of dollars on some glossy photocopied pieces of paper. This wasn't an isolated incident either. According to a news item I read on WTAW.com, a man from Dallas paid $1,700 to someone off craigslist for four tickets. After meeting the seller at a McDonald's in College Station, the tickets were revealed to be fraudulent when accessing the stadium.

As great as it was to be inside Kyle Field, there was still nearly two hours until the game was due to get underway. I mopped my brow with my 12th Man towel and considered how I'd go about chewing up the time. Surviving. That's how.

I located my seat in section 149 and baked in the sun for approximately eight seconds until I concluded that it wouldn't work until kickoff as a suitable pastime.

Whilst the minutes went by, the section filled up. I soon realized why my ticket had looked dissimilar to everyone else's. My ticket was for the "away section." Alabama fans surrounded me. At first I thought it might be fun and add a different element to my college football experience. And I'll tell you what, for the first two A&M offensive drives, I loved it as much as Sean Payton and his New Orleans Saints love drafting Heisman Trophy winning running backs.

Such a showpiece event wouldn't have been complete without Johnny being Johnny. Early in the second quarter, he pulled off a play that laughably defied the laws of probability, football and physics. With half a dozen bullish pass rushers bearing down on him, he threw a suicidal lobbed pass into the open backfield. With the whole stadium wide-eyed, out of nowhere, A&M's Edward Pope rose like a salmon to pluck the ball from thin air. As he crashed to the floor in a heap of Alabama defenders, the 12th Man's roar echoed all the way throughout the State of Texas. It truly summed up Johnny as a football player. Every coach in the world would have been screaming at him to throw the ball out of bounds to evade the sack. However, Manziel does not play by traditional norms and values. Instead he rolls the roulette wheel, lives on the edge and causes Coach Sumlin on the touchline to crack open another box of anti-heart attack medicine.

Sadly, as the saying goes, all good things come to an end. Alabama got their act together and marched down the field on repeat. Despite this, I continued to bellow my lungs dry as AJ McCarron prepared to take another snap.

The game finally came to a close and as much as I was distraught A&M had lost 49-42, I was proud. And that's what hit me the hardest.

Often sports are about winning and losing, but I felt differently. I left Kyle Field feeling upbeat and delighted I had witnessed a football game between two teams that could genuinely claim they are two of the best in the country—and it lived up to the hype.

Did I expect to feel like that? Of course not. I'd been in Aggieland for just a handful of weeks. Yet my bond with this team, university and township was stronger than I could have ever imagined.

It is a cliché that is often used. Once you go to Kyle Field, you never look back. You get the bug. Boy, did I have the bug.

13. THE BUCKET

I n the aftermath of the epic Alabama shootout, I could happily hold my hands up and admit that Aggieland had affected me in a way I never thought possible. The university, community and more importantly, the spirit, had convinced me that this place was truly one of a kind. Within a month, the color of my blood had turned into an Aggie shade of maroon.

Ultimately, the transformation reached a stage that it surprised me how strongly I felt about Texas A&M. For example, during one afternoon I was simply minding my own business when an ESPN segment popped up on TV. It was about how the Seattle Seahawks were attempting to become the loudest fans in the world. Pretty innocent, huh? Well, the news reporter kept referring to the Seahawks faithful as the "12th Man." A few weeks ago, I wouldn't have given it a second thought. Now, it royally ticked me off.

On the Sunday morning, the realization that 'Bama week had come to a close left me with a tinge of sadness. Those days leading up to the game will always stay with me. The buzz around College Station was unforgettable. How would future games ever compare? Especially as TV network, CBS, announced that the 'Bama showdown had earned the highest ratings for a CBS regular season college fixture in twenty-three years.

Fortuitously, I didn't have time to feel despondent. Jeff's partner in crime-fighting at the A&M Police Department, Tommy, had generously offered to take me to an NFL game in Houston to see the Texans take on the Tennessee Titans at Reliant Stadium.

When it came to the NFL, I had noticed the population of Aggieland was split. One half liked it and supported either the Cowboys or Texans. The other was so dedicated to A&M and university sports that they failed to have a good word to say about the professional stuff.

I'll be honest; my experiences of cities like Pittsburgh, New York and Washington, had led me to believe that the NFL was the big daddy. The King.

Not in Texas. Not in SEC country.

On one occasion, I fancied a trip to a local beer-selling establishment for a dabble in the weekly event known as NFL Thursday Night Football. Instead, what I got to see was the first half of a Texas Tech/TCU clash. Not a problem. We're in Texas, after all. As a polite Englishman, I wasn't about to throw my toys out the pram and insist that Tom Brady and Geno Smith should be put on display with immediate effect.

Someone else did, though. I gasped as a chap wearing a Boston Red Sox cap demanded the channel should be hastily changed. I continued to eat French fries. Following some toing and froing, he finally got his wish—albeit on a much smaller screen than the college game.

It was surprising to me that the amateur clash held more importance. Although with every day that went by, I shouldn't have been shocked by anything anymore.

Once Tommy picked me up, we started our trek towards the capital of humidity. This journey allowed me to take in more of the Texas landscape. It blew my mind that you'd drive for over an hour and be surrounded by baron land as far as the eye could see. Don't get me wrong. Britain has its fair share of countryside, but this was on another level. A few days before I'd heard someone on TV describe Texas as an "enormous farm"; I was starting to see where they were coming from!

Soon enough, after driving past a number of optimistic ticket scalpers, we arrived at Reliant Stadium. It made me chuckle how a group of these touts had an imposing sign with "TICKETS WANTED" scrawled across it and when someone stopped to sell some, they'd turn the sign around to reveal "TICKETS FOR SALE." They clearly ran a well-oiled ship.

As the infamous Astrodome stood in our vicinity, I finally got my first taste of tailgating. Tommy popped the trunk to reveal a glorious, icebox full of beers. With every sunken beverage, I came to the realization that I could certainly get used to this form of soaking up the pre-match atmosphere.

The college football and NFL gameday experiences were at polar opposites. At Kyle Field, everything is stripped back—as it should be. It is technically an amateur sport, after all. In some sections you stand for the whole game and if your legs tire, you have the option to sit on what I can only describe as a metal girder.

Reliant Stadium was different. The only time people got on their feet was when there was an important play, such as a touchdown or interception. Why stand up when you have a seat so comfortable it wouldn't look out of place in your front room? Oh, and when people are coming around every five minutes to sell you beer, what's not to love about that? Well, the fact they are $8 each, but that's a different story.

The atmosphere was much more volatile. I finally heard a string of profanities. It took me back to my first A&M game when I shouted a little something at a Rice running back. In this instance, a Houston fan nearby was giving Matt Shaub both barrels. It helped put things into perspective. Now I'm not saying that anyone deserves abuse to be hurled in their direction (well, there are some exceptions), but when you're being paid millions of dollars, do you really give a damn what some bozo holding a $16 corn dog thinks?

That's the fine line between the NFL and college. I now perfectly understood why the people that surrounded me at the Rice game reacted like they did. It just doesn't feel right taking out your frustrations on players that are essentially still kids.

Reliant's big plus point was something I hadn't foreseen— air conditioning. It was a lovely bowl of cool air. There wasn't someone passing out or sweating to death in sight. As aesthetically pleasing as it was, I couldn't help but feel the NFL continued its trend of portraying itself as an entity that's overly driven by money and sponsorship. For example, there were surreal announcements like: "If you look at the big screen in the next 1.3 seconds, you will win a footlong from Subway."

Now, don't get me wrong, I love a footlong (strictly a sandwich reference) as much as the next person, but the constant commercialization of the NFL can distract from what's important and the fundamental reason why you've turned up: the game of sport in front of you.

Yes, I initially discovered and fell in love with the NFL, but now I'd experienced both sides of the footballing coin, I was beginning to reevaluate. Stories such as the one I had labeled the "Case of the Tooth Fairy" came to mind. Earlier in the season, the Pittsburgh Steelers had paid kicker Shayne Graham $55,294 after being active on the roster for one measly game. During this clash he didn't even make it onto the field to swing his leg. Just imagine making that sort of moola for doing absolutely nothing. It reminded me of being a kid when you lose a tooth and get reimbursed—it's the easiest cash you ever make in your life.

Furthermore, halftime entertainment was something I'd never forget from my trip to Houston. After becoming accustomed to the best of the best in the form of The Fightin' Texas Aggie Band, Reliant Stadium delivered something at the other end of the spectrum—Vanilla Ice. His performance was on par with the actions of a nearby duo. These individuals were holding two signs. The first was a sizeable "D," and the other was a cutout graphic of a fence. It didn't take a rocket scientist to put the two together and see what they were conveying. Barmy.

On the whole, college football felt like a more authentic and genuine experience. It's more about the atmosphere, yells and players. You get more of a connection with the team at collegiate level, because they are representing a university, thousands of alumni and a close-knit community. They aren't multi-millionaires and don't embody a billion-dollar franchise that's being run by an egotistical billionaire.

For me, they both possessed their advantages and disadvantages. It really depends on what you prefer. I could see it from both sides, and my opinion had the potential to change with the more football games that I attended, but for now I simply loved American football—in every form.

On day one, God created the heavens, the earth, light and darkness.

On day two, God created tailgating.

Well, that's not strictly true.

However, after getting my first taste of this infamous and quintessential American pastime, Texas A&M-style, I reckon God probably saw it as a priority by at least day four or five.

From the moment I first set eyes on the hundreds of tailgaters swarming Kyle Field to the moment I got my first taste of drinking beer in the Reliant Stadium parking lot with Tommy, I knew it was time to immerse myself into this sacred activity.

It may or may not shock you to find out in the UK, we have nothing that even slightly resembles tailgating. In fact, if you are caught with a beer anywhere near a vehicle it's almost certain that you'll get arrested on suspicion of driving under the influence.

My only previous experience of witnessing tailgating in action before was at Heinz Field, Pittsburgh. On the way to the stadium you'd see hundreds of people huddling in parking lots, freezing their bottoms off in sub-zero temperatures and pissing into rusty timeworn buckets.

Tailgating in Texas was a different story. The only cold things you're likely to find are the elegant, cube-shaped blocks of ice that cuddle your unopened beers.

So, how was I going to arrive on the tailgating scene? Luckily, a friendly chap called Andy reached out to me and invited me along to the "Keep the Spirit Tailgate."

As I walked over to the west side of campus, I strolled through other tailgates. Judging by how plastered some people were, I imagined they'd probably commenced as early as 6:00 a.m.

What impressed me the most was seeing people set up. They'd reserved their spots as early as noon on the previous day. In some cases, it was a full-scale military operation. I watched as families carried pieces of furniture like coffee tables, dining room chairs and chandeliers. OK perhaps not chandeliers, but it was remarkable. I had visions of all the homes in a 100-mile radius around the Brazos Valley being completely empty because all of the furniture that sits in their house during the other six days of the week was now plonked outside Kyle Field.

I'd heard stories of how people go to football games and tailgate with RVs the size of mansions. Likewise, I'd seen BBQ grills at Reliant Stadium that were eight times bigger than my kitchen back home. As you'd walk past tailgate after tailgate, these grills kept getting bigger and bigger. It was as if there was an unspoken competition between them all to prove their masculinity through the size of their BBQ, which is fair enough—I'm the same with TVs. No joke, you could have a Picasso hanging on the wall of your living room, but the first thing I'll notice and judge is the size and wow factor that your television possesses. If your TV is a heap of junk, it's unlikely that I'll want to come and watch sports with you. In effect, this means there's basically zero chance we'll ever go the distance as friends. I'm never likely to be invited over to Jerry World, but if I was, you can bet a fair amount of cash on the fact I'd turn up. Yes, the dude appears to have his flaws. Regardless, if there's anyone that has taken putting a widescreen in their front room to the next level, it's Jezza. That Jumbotron seems to get bigger every time I see it. Televisions aside, it's time to get soppy and emotional. After tailgating for an hour or so, you quickly realize this activity is so much more than stuffing your face with as many chips as you humanly can, and drinking until you forget what direction the portable toilet is in.

It's a distinguished juncture that allows friends and families to get together, enjoy each other's company and have a laugh. Oh, and consume to your heart's content. There was no better indication of this when an hour before the game everyone congregated into a circle. The head of the Barnard family said some cordial words and thanked everyone for coming. Furthermore, people at the tailgate took it in turns each week to weigh in with some wholehearted and profound verses, such as the following from an Aggie named Derek:

> *Here's to all the Ags I know, and those I've yet to meet.*
> *The ones I can't wait for Saturday, to show up and greet.*
> *Some by plane and some by car, some from near and some from far.*
> *Some climbed on stack, some drive us home. But it's always here we return. No matter where we've roamed.*
> *You see, our locked arms are a symbol, of our strength when we're together.*
> *Because when that 12th Man stands at ready, it's clear there is no better.*
> *Everyone here circled now, surely knows that Aggie spirit, but it's when we stand to saw 'em off, well that's when the whole damn world will hear it.*
> *And surely there are those who just don't get our ways, but I'll tell you what, you dirty hippies, Highway 6... It runs both ways!*

A bucket is then handed around with everyone taking turns to drink from it. What was in it? Probably a potent mixture of vodka and tears of Texas Longhorns. Later on, I learned the bucket originated from an old lady that walked around tailgates at Aggies' road games many years ago. She distributed the bucket, but was never seen again. Chris Barnard had since taken the torch and transformed it into an integral part of their tailgating tradition.

Next door, there was a modified school bus that had been dubbed "The 12th Van." Judging by the title of this book, you can tell I love a pun as much as anyone, so they had me at hello. I quickly noticed they had Newcastle Brown Ale on tap—an English beer. I was astounded. You'd do well to find that stuff at home, especially in the south. So, to find a keg of it sat in a nifty modified school bus on the other side of the Atlantic took me by surprise.

The final detail that left me flabbergasted was how anyone plucks up the motivation to attend the sporting event that everyone has assembled for. The temptation to sit in a comfy seat and watch the football on an outside screen whilst continuing to indulge was almost too much. Eventually, I hauled myself to the stadium—with beer in hand.

After battling the temptation to continue tailgating, there was a game to be watched. SMU. I'll put my cards on the table and admit that during the game I had absolutely no idea what SMU stood for. All I had was a confident hunch that the "U" stood for university.

I could have looked it up or asked someone, but to be honest it's not like I had a burning desire to find out. It's like a hamburger I once purchased from a mysterious van outside of Aston Villa's soccer stadium. The bread tasted like bread. Inside it? Certainly not beef, or meat. Hunger encapsulated me. In that moment nothing else mattered. It was food. Had it broken advertisement laws? Possibly. It certainly wasn't a burger in the conventional sense. But it did the job; it filled me up. The mystery of not knowing appealed to me more than exploring the inconvenient truth.

Am I implying that SMU is like a dodgy burger? Don't be silly; they aren't Longhorns. But following the immense highs and lows of the previous week against Alabama, I couldn't help but think this game needed all the mystery, excitement and references to illegitimate meat products it could get.

The day before the contest, the rain came. I'd experienced the soaring Texan heat, but now it was time to rock a poncho. On my walk back to my swanky travel tavern, the rain pelted down. In England this is something that happens at least four times a day. I'll tell you what though, Texan Rain 1-0 English Rain. Rain in Texas is warmer. So, even when you're getting drenched you're not freezing your gonads off at the same time.

With the rain came the belief that midnight yell practice might be abandoned. I gave Jeff a quick call and asked if it was still on. He laughed at me down the phone for three minutes and hung up. He later told me he'd been working at A&M for over 20 years and had never seen a yell practice scrapped.

In contrast to the week before, three quarters of the student section's bottom tier was filled—it was still impressive dedication for a damp squib.

Game day. As I walked to the stadium, I hadn't given much thought to where my seat would be located. All I knew was I'd be up with the Gods at the top of the stand that overlooks the north end zone.

The very moment I entered the ramp it was as if I'd joined a swirling vortex. You seem to walk in a circle for hours until you finally get to the very top of the structure. I took a moment to compose myself as I dealt with a brutal case of dizziness, fear of heights and general lack of fitness.

Once I'd gotten myself together it was time to locate my seat. I prayed I'd be low down. I looked at my ticket hoping to see any number between 1 and 5. Nope. Row 33. Kyle Field was quickly becoming my Mount Everest. I continued to climb until I reached the summit. I sat there for a moment simply taking in the incredible view of College Station. For a split-second, I thought I could perhaps see my homeland in the distance.

Compared to the three previous games, this matchup seemed harder to get into. Was it because I'd usually sat much closer to the field? Or perhaps it was because after the experience of 'Bama, nothing would ever quite reach that tipping point again. Whatever it was, it did have an eerie feeling of a hangover from the week before.

Nonetheless, in the first half A&M was still in the mood to pile a considerable amount of points on the board. Even though I felt uneasy standing so high up, I braved getting to my feet on regular occasions. I won't lie; I had visions of misjudging how much I'd enjoyed the tailgate, drunkenly falling over and tumbling to the bottom of the steep tier—vanishing into a cloud of smoke.

Malcome Kennedy had a standout game for the Aggies, and topped off the evening's shenanigans with a lavish touchdown. Unfortunately, the afternoon wasn't as memorable for A&M's kicker, Taylor Bertolet. After admirably recovering his own onside kick earlier in the clash, he had a terrible time of converting some elementary kicks. Coach Sumlin soon lost patience and ended up replacing him with backup kicker, Josh Lambo.

It was deep into the fourth quarter. All game I had been subjected to a young lad sitting behind me who at a guess, was seven years old. He asked his dad a question every 3.7 seconds. Now, don't get me wrong, I think it's important kids should attend football matches. The bond that sports can create between father and son is unbreakable. Besides, I couldn't really talk because I was still a relative newbie when it came to football, so I, too, was asking similarly inane questions not so long ago. However, when you've sat through nearly three hours of it, your threshold slowly evaporates. And with one more question, I lost the will to live. And it will stay with me forever.

"Daddy, if a field goal kick is like really, really good, and I mean twice the distance than one usually is, can the referee think *woah! That's impressive!* And give a touchdown?"

I got up and left.

During previous games I'd sat right in the corner of the Jumbotron end zone. From that viewpoint you can see dozens of people that come to games, sit on the artificial lawn, and watch the action on the big screen. This always made me curious. What's the point of coming to a sporting event just to watch it on a massive television? The thought crossed my mind that perhaps these individuals don't own televisions and are really impressed with the advanced technology.

Anyway, as soon as I left sitting in a cloud, I thought if you can't beat them, or understand them, you might as well join them. So I did exactly that. After making the long walk to the other side of the complex and taking a knee in front of the scarily large display, I was even more baffled.

My eyes. Oh, my eyes. As it was dark, the screen seemed ten times brighter than usual. I felt the colors and images burning into my vision. I'll be honest; I didn't care for it much, but it did help me to gain an understanding behind why people go there. It's usually families with small kids that probably find it an easy way to keep tabs on everything whilst sampling the gameday experience.

It had a further surprise up its sleeve. I saw someone eating what I can only describe as a slop of meat plastered onto a mound of nachos. I'd easily say it was one of the least appetizing things I'd ever seen. And yet, I couldn't take my eyes off the person devouring it. He wolfed it down without a care in the world. On the surface, I was wincing. But deep inside, I was impressed. If someone put that on a plate in front of me and said they'd give me a thousand bucks if I ate it all, I'm not sure I could.

I'd noticed halfway through the fourth quarter that Kyle Field was looking empty. I'll admit that the last quarter wasn't particularly pleasant viewing, but it surprised me. This was until I remembered there were effectively hundreds of small pubs in the form of tailgates located around the stadium that people were flocking to. I was tempted to join them, but just about hung onto the final play of A&M's 42-13 victory.

Regrettably when planning my stay in Aggieland, my budget wouldn't stretch as far as staying at the Ritz. Not that there is one, anyway. Instead, following deep deliberation and a few glances on Google, I ended up choosing a picturesque, charming and more importantly cost-effective, travel tavern.

I now found myself packed and ready to nip back to England for a brief spell. With this in mind, would I miss the unrivaled luxury of my beloved quarters? For starters, on a daily basis I'd been given all the mini-soaps, shampoos and conditioners that I could ever dream of. Genuine question—What more could a man want?

Well, this place had the answer. Towels, towels and more towels. I'd never seen so many different sizes of towel. Big, really big, small, and medium. I had no idea why I had been supplied with such a broad range of dimensions, and the majority of me was satisfied with not knowing.

I had quickly turned into an American version of Alan Partridge. When bored of President Palmer from *24* asking me, "Are you in good hands?" on yet another Allstate Insurance commercial, I seriously considered taking the trouser press apart just so I could put it back together for something to do. Instead, I favored a game that I devised in my spare time. This was seeing if I could throw a water bottle (empty of course—for health and safety reasons) into a bin that's located at the other side of the room. I think it's fair to say I know how to party.

Unluckily, it hadn't all been strippers, revelry and events organized by Charlie Sheen. Two days before the Alabama game, something peculiar happened. Whilst brushing my teeth, an exotic noise boomed throughout the air. I was startled as I realized that someone was ringing the room's prehistoric telephone. A grainy voice greeted me—it was a person claiming to work for the travel tavern. I wondered whether they were going to complain about Charlie's tiger blood that was maturing in the sink. To cut a long story short, it was a rascal claiming I'd used up my entire internet and TV allocation, and was now demanding my credit card details to reactivate both. Fortunately, I saw through his devious plan and chucked various expletives in his direction. In the aftermath, I was relieved to get confirmation at reception that it was indeed a con artist trying his luck. Nice try, Sonny Jim.

On a brighter note, with my pending return to the UK, I was complacent with the knowledge I'd soon be able to console myself with a generous helping of home-cooked grub. It took until my third week before I finally prepared a meal myself. Shocking, I know, but it's not my fault that eating out holds such temptation. On this fateful occasion I visited the nearby HEB supermarket and let loose. I'd made the biggest rookie error of them all—food shopping on an empty stomach.

Everything looked appealing. I hadn't even covered half the ground and my basket was overflowing with stuff I'd probably never get around to eating. Another obvious error was waiting for me around the corner. I had bought the ingredients to make myself a lovely, homemade, ham and cheese bloomer. As I got back to my room, devastation ensued. The realization I had zero kitchen utensils started to set in.

In the end I had to make do with the cards I'd been dealt. I hacked open the bread with my bare hands, and quickly stuffed it with ham and cheese. I then ate it in a speedy fashion before all the contents fell out. Very gourmet.

Once I was fed and watered, I got back to watching one of the ten billion US and Mexican TV channels that I had the delight of choosing from. Over the weeks some shows I'd watched left me with more questions than answers. For instance, ESPN broadcasts sports such as Live Poker and full unedited recaps of the 2012 Little League Baseball World Series. Now, I'd perfectly understood a number of cultural differences since arriving. On the other hand, I couldn't help but try and work out who exactly was watching these 11- to 13-year-olds playing baseball with a real interest? Apart from the families of the kids that are involved, what is the appeal? Are people tailgating outside? I couldn't figure it out.

Subsequently, I soon found myself flicking through waves of Spanish soap operas and reality dross. During one afternoon I was lucky enough to discover a program that was solely dedicated to the Dallas Cowboys cheerleaders. Again, my opinion of Jerry Jones improved.

The biggest drawback of watching US television is that it turns you into a hypochondriac. There are medical commercials on every five minutes that list 20-30 things that could potentially go wrong with you if you decide to take the medication they are trying to flog. Why anyone would then think about rushing to the store and purchasing it completely boggles my mind. I'm not even joking; one commercial about sleeping pills listed a potential drawback as possible death.

Talking of possible death, I'd soon be hopping on a plane back to England. Following a fairly quiet final night in "C-Stat," it was time to get ready to return to my homeland.

14. Gunspoint

T he first leg of my Aggieland adventure was complete.

As I exited the Brazos Valley, I was feeling an assortment of emotions. Yes, I was happy to head home to see family and friends. However, a bulky portion of my existence did not want to leave.

On the journey to Houston, I began to reflect on my adventure thus far. So many unique and special memories came flooding back. Whether it was my first midnight yell or the time I walked down South Texas Avenue and nearly died from dehydration, I reminisced with great fondness.

This wasn't goodbye. In just a couple of weeks I'd be back on the terraces of Kyle Field, slapping my bicep and shouting about how farmers love to fight.

In this moment, my number one priority was getting home in one piece. First off, a night in Houston awaited before flying back to London. I had presumed this stopover would go smoothly. It didn't. It merely added to my roller-coaster of fun, emotion and lunacy.

After politely thanking the Ground Shuttle driver for dropping me off at Terminal C of George Bush Intercontinental Airport, I was on my own. With the sun glazing my lightly burned skin, I quickly surveyed the area for the nearest taxi rank. There she was, in all her glory.

A queue had formed. This allowed me enough time to reach into my white Adidas satchel and obtain the address of the hotel I was due to stay in.

Soon enough it was my turn to inelegantly slide into the back of a cab.

"Where would you like to go?" enquired the driver.

Without hesitation, I handed over a scroll of parchment that contained the required details and zip code. A murky quietness filled the air. He scrutinized the document and shot me a look that suggested I was asking for a ride to Outer Mongolia.

To my surprise, he opened his door and exited the vehicle.

"Oi mate, where are you going?" I squealed.

Whilst waving my document around like it was an evil artifact, he meandered over to a taxi guru that sat in the shadows of a small wooden hut. I was puzzled. To be honest, I hadn't given this hotel a second thought since the day I booked it back in England. I vaguely remembered making the reservation whilst Expedia was running an offer on airport hotels. Needless to say, I found myself typing in "Houston airport hotel" and booking the cheapest one available.

I'll happily hold my hands up and admit to loving a bargain. In fact, I probably take it a little too far. For example, there is a parking lot near my residency that charges extortionate rates 364 days a year. However, on Christmas Day they let you in for free. Consequently, as other people are looking forward to a day of fun festivities, I've got my eyes firmly fixed on the parking space prize. You simply can't miss such open goals.

This perceived illness brings out another trait of mine—getting my money's worth. I wouldn't think twice about spending an hour squeezing the last particle of toothpaste out of its tube, or refusing to get a haircut until my hair is so long that I begin to resemble an overgrown bear. As a result, I was hopeful that my budget Expedia hotel would prove to be the type of colossal deal that I could smile about for years to come.

Clearly, something about this hotel had ruffled the feathers of the driver. Eventually he came back to the car and hurriedly entered the zip code into his robust, satellite navigation system. I breathed a sigh of relief. It seemed the controversy of my pending location had settled down.

Fifteen minutes later, my optimism started to shrink again. Whilst the meter kept going up and up, it was evident that we were driving miles away from the airport. This wasn't the only worry. As soon as we turned off the main highway, the driver asked me the question that no taxi passenger should ever hear.

"Where is this place?"

I almost laughed out loud.

"Do I know where it is? I've never been around here in my life!"

At least I'd discovered the reason why he was making such a fuss when I first handed him the address.

Once we had driven down six or seven dead ends, he made an executive judgment to rejoin the highway and get off at the next exit. The decision paid off. The hotel was in the distance. I'd never seen a cabbie punch the air with such joy.

As frustrated as I was with paying a considerable amount of dosh for a taxi journey in which I received an undesired tour of a suburb's backstreets, I was relieved to finally make it to my desired location.

My first impressions of my forthcoming abode were not positive. Unbearable noise and fumes occupied the air. The hotel was situated underneath one of the biggest highway interchanges on the planet. Also, it looked like something out of a CSI TV show. It was a stereotypical set up with high-rising rooms overlooking a misty and gloomy swimming pool.

Not wanting to hang out in the open for much longer, I quickly made my way to reception. Apart from wanting to charge me twice for a prepaid room, the checking in process went by without a hitch. Before I knew it, I was in my room watching the early Sunday NFL games on a thirty-year-old television.

By this point I fancied a mid-afternoon nap. The bed was like nothing I'd ever experienced. For some unknown reason it had large wheels on each of the corners. Whenever I moved, the bed shuffled a couple of yards along the floor. It was the equivalent of sleeping on an enthusiastic skateboard.

With my nap out of the way, it was time to find somewhere that sold necessities such as food and drink. I only had half a bottle of water and three Oreos remaining in my stash. My first idea was to look up the hotel on Google Maps to see if there was anywhere nearby. No matter how many times I zoomed in on the buildings that surrounded this place, none of them popped up with names I recognized as somewhere that potentially served dinner. Oh, how I longed for a burrito and gigantic tub of queso from Freebirds. In the end, I clicked on a hideout that was a quarter of a mile away. It claimed to be a bar. Surely they do grub? Without hesitation I seized my belongings and set off on a quest to find something edible.

An unfriendly combination of humidity and air pollution did its best to try and slow me down. Ultimately, I reached this potential food-selling establishment.

Before I entered I couldn't help but notice the other shops that surrounded the vacant parking lot I was standing in. The one that stood out the most was "LINDSAY'S LINGERIE." Automatically, I had two questions. Who is Lindsay and why is she selling her underwear?

As I was so hungry, I wasn't in the mood to dwell on such uncertainties for much longer and finally entered the bar. The first features that struck me was how unoccupied and poorly lit it was. My entrance had doubled the attendance. I guessed it was quiet because most people were probably next door checking out Lindsay's reasonably priced under garments.

Regardless, I maintained my composure. Once I had ordered a drink, I bravely asked the barmaid if they served food.

"The kitchen is closed until later."

"Any idea what time?" I asked.

She shrugged her shoulders.

My stomach ached with hunger. Luckily, after a couple of beers my concentration was focused towards the Indianapolis Colts vs. San Francisco 49ers game that was being broadcasted on an acceptable-sized monitor. One aspect I couldn't ignore was how empty this place was. It was a large bar and I was only accompanied by one other person, who I firmly suspected was the bar owner. Moreover, I had made a staggering discovery—a large pole in the middle of the room. It didn't require a genius to work out what this pole was usually used for.

Following one more beer, I determined it was time to move on. Before it got dark I wanted to see if there were any other options further down the road. Within a hundred yards it was plain to see there was nothing. If I wanted to eat tonight, I'd have to pray that the mystical chef in the bar fancied powering up the oven.

Not knowing when the kitchen would be open, if at all, I concluded that I should return to the hotel and polish off my last three biscuits. The idea of revisiting the bar didn't bother me much. After all, my Pittsburgh Steelers were playing the Chicago Bears in NFL Sunday Night Football, and even in a completely empty bar the atmosphere ought to be an improvement on watching it in black and white whilst lying on a glorified skateboard.

A couple of hours passed. It was time to depart my dog basket-like habitation and start praying the bar's kitchen was ready to solve my starvation.

On my approach to the parking lot, I immediately sensed that something didn't quite add up. Previously, there were less than five cars parked. Now there wasn't an empty space in sight. In reality, the parking lot was so oversubscribed that people had abandoned their modes of transport in areas that weren't even designated spaces.

Before I could contemplate the parking restrictions and hand out some potential ticket-saving advice, I noticed a plethora of individuals dismounting from their motorbikes. For some unknown reason they were looking at me in an ominous fashion. Despite this, I didn't give it much thought. My focus was purely down to getting food into my belly.

When I arrived at the entrance, I noticed someone holding the front door open. My initial thought was "Hooray! More people! I'm not going to be on my own!" Curiously, the fact he was wearing a New England Patriots jersey with Aaron Hernandez's name plastered on the back barely registered.

As I entered I was in complete shock. It was absolutely packed. In the space of two hours I'd gone from being their only customer to visiting the bar and finding a six-deep queue.

The next realization that hastily became apparent was why the people outside had given me bemused looks. I was the only white person in the whole building. At first, I tried to ignore this glaring statistic.

During my patient wait for a pint of their finest and most competitively priced lager, I noticed a Hispanic gentleman wearing a Pittsburgh Steelers cap. In an attempt to break the ice in this unexpected scenario, I went over and tried to drum up a conversation about the Steelers' precarious running back situation. When this resulted in little response, I resorted to bringing up the plaguing issues on the offensive line and asked him, "Should we really be relying on a 7th round draft pick to play left tackle?"

Deafening silence. He could not have looked any less interested in the words spewing out of my nervous lips.

Shortly afterwards, it became apparent that my attempts at conversation had not gone unnoticed. A threatening, well-built alpha male in bike leathers menacingly approached me.

"You lost, brah?"

Hmm. Why was he calling me a bra? Was he getting me mixed up with Lindsay? Clearly, I didn't have the bollocks to say that to him.

"Erm, I've come here for something to eat."

Without fail, he latched onto the English accent.

"You're not from around here, are you?" he retorted.

"No." I shakily replied.

He walked off and whispered an abundance of sweet nothings into the ears of his clan. I was on the brink of crapping myself. Was he going to return? A further observation was that he wasn't the only one wearing bike leathers. In fact, 95% of people were either wearing them or tattooed up to their eyeballs. I'd literally entered Houston's version of Sons of Anarchy.

My mind was racing. What the hell should I do? With a glimpse of something, my decision was made for me. An intimidating bald fellow to my left had a gun holstered. I could safely say this was the first firearm I'd seen outside of my Call of Duty online gaming community.

Once I clocked it, f*** that. I was out of there, especially when I noticed plenty of other weapons dotted around the place. My conundrum was, how do I exit in a polite and controlled manner so it doesn't look like I'm fleeing the scene? I quickly thought on my feet as the man that called me a bra came bustling back towards me.

Panic stations. Ahh, what props did I have at my disposal? Phone! My phone! I pretended it was ringing and that I couldn't hear what the caller on the other end of the line was saying. I made it look like I was exiting through the back door in a bid to find somewhere quieter. As I accelerated away from the bar, I glanced over my shoulder. To my complete horror, the bike-leathered lothario that I'd vocalized with had followed me out into the open. I didn't dare look back as I sprinted as fast as I humanly could back to my hotel.

I slammed the door shut. Adrenaline coursed through my veins. For several minutes in that bar, all eyes were on me. I genuinely didn't feel safe.

The next morning I was weak and grumpy. The thought of my pending ten-hour plane journey back to the UK twisted and turned my empty paunch. Nevertheless, I wanted to get out of the hotel as soon as possible.

Whilst striding to reception to check out, I couldn't help but notice an ominous looking shape floating in the swimming pool. It looked suspiciously like a body. I froze as I zoomed in on the object. Without delay, it became apparent it was actually a blow-up sex doll. Evidently, Lindsay didn't just sell lingerie next door. The most harrowing part of the doll's existence was the potential back-story. How on earth did it get there? Did someone have a 'go' on it? In the aftermath, did they try and dispose of the evidence by throwing it in the pool? Whatever it was, unsurprisingly I didn't hang around to find out.

Even though I wasn't looking forward to the flight, I had never been so pleased to see an airport before. I whizzed through customs and found a thin slice of heaven in the form of a Ruby's Diner. Without hesitation, a burger, fries and chocolate milkshake were thrown down my neck at an exhilarating speed. Color began to show in my cheeks again.

Basking in such ecstasy, the words of the taxi driver that had delivered me to the airport started to play on my mind.

"How come you chose to stay in Greenspoint? You do realize it's known as Gunspoint, don't you?"

I did now.

15. BACK IN BLIGHTY

Acclimatizing to the British Isles proved to be difficult. For example, I soon learned it's heavily frowned upon if you accidentally try and purchase a bacon and egg sandwich with US dollars.

Such slip-ups were occurring because from the moment I landed in London, I was counting down the days until my return to College Station. From the creaking trains that I had no idea where they were going, to people saying, "What? Like the Governor?" every time I informed someone of my surname, I missed everything about Aggieland.

Seeing friends and family helped to take my mind off such heartache. However, all of their questions understandably followed a similar path. They wanted the scoop on Texas. My first response was always the same: it's nothing like I imagined.

In England, there is a defined portrait of the deep south of America. There was a *Top Gear* episode that aired in 2007, which saw the crew drive around the south with slogans such as "Man-love Rules," "Country and Western is Rubbish," "Hillary for President" and "NASCAR Sucks" painted on their cars. Yes, that is British humor. They were pelted with rocks and chased down the highway.

Someone reminded me of that episode and it stuck with me. I remembered watching it and naively thought everyone there must be bloody crazy. Now? I had people that I considered family and lifelong friends in Texas.

Yes, I came across people that were different to anyone I'd ever met before. In Northgate, I once offended someone by accidentally dropping an "F bomb" into conversation. In my defense, I had guzzled half a dozen beers and contain the heavy burden of possessing a monumental potty mouth.

Regardless, does it fit the stereotype that was portrayed? Not at all. The people of Texas are the definition of caring, amicable and considerate (except when they are shouting at pedestrians from behind a steering wheel). It saddened me coming back to the UK and resorting to the normal routine. No one says hello or asks how you are. Quite simply, people are more than happy to live in a tunnel vision society.

I'll admit that sometimes I felt like an alien in Aggieland. Every day I tripped over a bevy of charming, unconventional and spellbinding nuances. For instance, an on-looking stranger out of nowhere informed me that the combination of waffles and fried chicken is an integral Texan delicacy. Soon enough, I chomped down a plateful of this refined grub. I was impressed—remarkably, these two unexpected components complimented each other in a way I never thought possible. From that day onwards, waffles were added to my daily staple diet.

Away from food, memories of when I first heard the cannon at Kyle Field came flooding back. Explaining to my peers that a cannon is set off during games and at midnight yell was hard enough. Midnight yell, you say? I almost didn't bother. That absolutely blew their minds. After all, it blew mine the first time I experienced it. I gave them the brief details. The moment I saw their faces when I let them know 50,000 people had turned up for the Alabama practice, I knew I had to stop. That alone made them think I was manipulating the truth. With this in mind, I didn't delve too deeply into the park rangers with horses that are dressed like they've just come straight off the television set of *Deep South*.

"Bet you love the cheerleaders though!" was a response I received. They immediately recoiled when I told them A&M is one of the only college football teams that do not have cheerleaders.

"You traveled all that way for no cheerleaders? Are you mad?"

As if leaving everything behind for college football wasn't already an indication of madness, but apparently a lack of cheerleaders was the tipping point.

Taking this into consideration, I tried my best to convey other traditions. A big one is not exclusive to A&M, but to college football as a whole—the marching band. I'll lay my cards on the table here and honestly, if you're a current/ex member of the band, please don't be offended. This is purely an unfortunate detail across the pond. Marching bands such as the one we see at Kyle Field do not exist in England. Why don't they? Well, I'll tell you from personal experience. During my school years, the band or choir was perhaps the un-coolest thing you could be a part of. Anyone that had any connection to music or drama had their sexuality placed under a substantial microscope.

And yet, different cultures, different societies, different activities prosper. Aspects like that were exactly why I wanted to portray the story of Aggieland and college football from an outsider's point of view. The Fightin' Texas Aggie Band was one of the most spine-tingling, memorable and special things that I experienced in College Station. From hearing them approach Kyle Field for midnight yell, hearing THAT tune, to playing at half time, they make you feel at home. Also, in the aftermath of each game, I found myself continuously humming, "Hullabaloo, Caneck! Caneck!"

When it came to the hardest trait I had to convey, it wasn't fish camp, the UT rivalry or the cannon. It was Reveille.

Before I flew out to Texas, I knew college football had a strong affinity with mascots. I had heard Baylor University ran a black bear program that saw them represented by a couple of North American black bears. Real bears! At a sporting event? Speechless.

Once I initially came across Texas A&M, I noticed their mascot was a Rough Collie called Reveille. My reaction was snap; the mascot of my soccer team is also a dog. That is where the comparisons abruptly end.

Portsmouth's Nelson is a six-foot male dressed in a poorly made dog's costume. Why is he called Nelson? Because he's named in honor of the famous British Naval admiral, Admiral Horatio Nelson. The team is based in the most prestigious naval city in the country.

A few years after being introduced, he was even given a wife—Mary Rose. She was named in conjunction with a ship that was active in the 16th century. Again, she is merely a bloke that drew a short straw in life and ended up dressing as a dog for a living.

So, the fact A&M was using a real pooch was a preliminary surprise. But that was nothing until I found out that "Rev" isn't just a dog. She is the highest-ranking member of the Texas A&M Corps of Cadets, and is known as the first lady of Aggieland.

Imagine explaining that to someone that's used to a mascot being a guy you have a couple of beers with after a game while he's still wearing half a dog's costume? I barely managed it. At A&M this was real and Reveille is more than a mascot—she is a symbol of Aggie football.

When I picture my soccer team, do I ever think of the unfortunate chap dressed as a dog? Of course not. Yet when it comes to A&M, the reception Reveille gets says it all.

Whilst explaining this, people were in disbelief. It's not comprehensible in England. Especially once I explained there is a mascot corporal that has the sole responsibility of caring for her. This person has to take Reveille literally everywhere, including class and on dates.

When I was initially informed of this, I had to get confirmation at least seven times. On dates? Excuse me? I bet the guy that looks after her isn't short of offers. I bet he gives it the big one.

"Do you know who I am? I am Reveille's daddy!"

It probably works for him every time. Guaranteed success. That's not all. If Reveille decides to sleep on a cadet's bed, they must sleep on the floor. Likewise, if you're in a class and she barks while the professor is teaching, class is immediately canceled. In truth, the more I consider it; Reveille's story is a sitcom waiting to be written. I call shotgun on the rights.

I'll hold my hands up and admit there was still plenty of stuff I didn't fully understand. For example, during my first few outings to Kyle Field, I couldn't get my head around why people kept making "pretend guns" with their hands. In the aftermath of each yell, 87,000 people clasped their hands together into a gun shape and fired into the sky accompanied with a "Whoop!" Did I join in with it? Of course! After all, it reminded me of playing make-believe shooting games with my friends when I was younger, and that's never a bad thing.

Finally, the last feature that took me by surprise was the phenomenon known as the "high five." I bet you're thinking: "What? You're joking, right?" Nope. At soccer games when your team scores everyone goes absolutely mental. And when I mean mental, you will hug and embrace every stranger in your vicinity. If you even attempted to high five someone, they'd look at you like you're from Planet Zog. In the US, the high five is the socially acceptable way to celebrate. The first game against Rice after a touchdown, someone threw up their hand; I genuinely had no idea what to do with it. Do I shake it? Eventually, I worked out that a flat palm surely means high five territory. From then onwards, I was sorted.

And that's as much as I was willing to share. I could have explained stuff in more detail, like letting them know what a "koozie" is. Additionally, I could have told them how the staff at Kyle Field do a twirl and shout "EXACT CHANGE!" when you hand over precisely the right amount of currency. But for their safety and for mine, I didn't think they were quite ready for it yet.

In the past, every time I would hear someone complain about jet lag, I'd usually tell them to grow a pair and get on with it. I will never do that again.

Once I returned to the UK, my sleeping pattern was as erratic as Taylor Bertolet's kicking. Each day it felt like my head was being repeatedly sat on by Houston Texans' defensive end, J. J. Watt.

Subsequently, when it came to my homecoming weekend, I was in a sorry state. It's fair to say that the tired version of myself is something I need to assess and improve.

On the Friday night I barely slept at all. Lying there when you know you have zero chance of nodding off has to be one of the most frustrating things on this planet. Yet I did for hours. I tried everything apart from counting sheep. That is far too cliché for my liking. In its place I attempted tried and tested methods, such as reciting Portsmouth FC jersey numbers from the 1998 and 1999 seasons to myself. OK, I probably shouldn't have shared that—it looks weird written down.

Ultimately, I gave up and grumpily marched to the living room where I took residence on the couch. I flicked between TV channels until I settled on a hard-hitting documentary, *The Cove*. For someone that was trying to find something to aid sleepy thoughts, I should never have watched it. In hindsight, I'm glad I did. If you've never heard about it, you have to see it. It's about an appalling seaside village in Japan that sees thousands of dolphins slaughtered in secret every year, yet no one is doing diddly-squat about it. So, instead of sending me to the land of nod, it made me even more awake. I spent the next couple of hours signing petitions and reading every available snippet on the subject.

The morning soon came; I had a dreary, floaty feeling of exhaustion. I had no choice but to battle through. Me, Katie and her newly acquired designer handbag from T.J. Maxx were due to go to London and attend an NFL UK street party that was being put on to promote the following day's Steelers-Vikings NFL International Series game at Wembley.

In the back of my mind I knew Texas A&M had a late kick-off at midnight UK time. On one hand this was good, because I'd be home by then and could watch it. However, it looked doubtful I'd still be awake at 8:00 p.m. let alone reach kickoff.

In the morning, once I got to the train station, desperate times called for desperate measures. I bought a large can of

Red Bull. I was counting on it to make me feel human again. It did not. All it did was remind me of the sickly-taste it provided when mixed with vodka, as that used to be a regular tipple of mine at university. This was perhaps the last thing I needed.

Finally, my mood improved. It was probably the five or six jars of British ale that cheered me up. By this point I'd almost given up on being able to stay up for A&M's clash against Arkansas. After all, alcohol doesn't exactly help retain consciousness.

We left Central London at 10:00 p.m. As long as I stayed awake on the train, I fancied my chances to watch at least the first half. Any hiccups such as a quick nap signaled game over.

The whole way the train felt like it was going three miles per hour. As I willed myself to stay awake, I equally wished the train driver would put his foot down so I could rush home, have a cold shower and watch Johnny Football eat bacon for dinner.

At last the train pulled into our stop. All I had now was a straightforward ten-minute walk to the apartment. The fresh air combined with dozens of boozy revelers arguing, fighting and urinating in the street seemed to heighten my senses.

I'd come this far. I wasn't going to throw my 12th Man towel in now. No way. I was going to stay up for the whole game.

Early in the showdown, it proved to be an excellent decision. Trey Williams was swiftly becoming one of my favorite players as he rattled through the Arkansas defense and finished the game with a mouth-watering average of 9.2 yards per carry. Meanwhile, Johnny Manziel and Mike Evans continued their telepathic understanding that basically reached the point of Johnny hurtling the ball in Mike's general direction and having full confidence that it would result in a lofty completion. To use an NFL comparison, it was like watching Drew Brees and Jimmy Graham in New Orleans. Ironically in both duos, the quarterbacks are similar in stature and the two receivers are former basketball players. Coach Sumlin, you can have that blueprint for success free of charge. Don't worry about it, this one's on me.

In total, I struggled to stay awake here and there (especially during halftime), but eventually; I made it to the end. At 3:23 a.m. the day was over. The Aggies had beaten Arkansas 45-33, and the menacing pig etched into the middle of the field was now merely reduced to a withered ham and lettuce sandwich. I drifted off and dreamed about Deshazor Everett's momentum-shifting pick-six.

After four consecutive weekends of watching college football, I probably wasn't in the right frame of mind for an NFL International Series game. I'm not overly sure what I made of it.

Half of me thought it was great fun and we should love having any type of American Football that we can get our grubby English paws on. The other half was relatively cynical; in the same way I was during the Texans game I attended in Houston.

On the Saturday, Regent Street was closed so that an NFL fan rally could take place. There was a main stage that saw former players introduced and paraded like God-like figures in front of hundreds of thousands of people. As a positive, it provided British fans a taste of something that isn't particularly accessible on the right-hand side of the Atlantic.

So why the cynicism? At times I felt like I was in a commercial, cheesy and patronizing bubble that was trying to ram a sport down our throats at a ridiculous pace. Instead of trying to attract new fans, all we were to the NFL was an attempt to make another dollar or two. I could rant about that for a while, but rather than bore the tits off you, I shall humbly admit that it backed up what I was beginning to feel anyway. I was coming around to the idea that the college version of the game is superior. If anything, this occasion made that belief even stronger.

At Kyle Field, are you badgered to go to the megastore and buy, buy, buy every five minutes? College football is a more stripped back, authentic and unique occasion. In my opinion, it clearly matters to the fans and players more.

Don't get me wrong; I still loved the NFL and found it invigorating, but the huge focus on making as much money as possible is what made me become disillusioned with soccer. Maybe that's the direction sports are going in these days and I have to live with it. Who knows?

Anyway, the actual gameday was much better. It seemed far less tacky and we had a game to watch. Similarly, I enjoyed observing how different the atmosphere was. Where I was sitting, it was obvious that a majority of people were also soccer fans. This was evident because of the type of songs and cheers that accompanied the on-field events. It really was a bizarre mix of the two cultures. For example, a group to my left sarcastically jeered "WHEEEEY!" in unison as Vikings wide receiver, Greg Jennings, embarrassingly dropped a pass. That's a typical soccer reaction, and I recalled doing exactly the same thing on my first visit to Kyle Field. The difference was that I was the only one doing it.

On the way to Wembley, I saw all 32 NFL team jerseys on display and to my disgust, I saw one idiot wearing a Texas

Longhorns t-shirt. Yes, I was tempted to throw my sizzling hot pie at him.

Sooner or later, the game came and went. My Steelers had just lost their fourth game in a row and I was feeling miserable.

As I made my way back to the tube station, in the corner of my eye I saw the number 12 on the back of someone's attire. Instinctively, I thought, surely not? But hallelujah, praise the lord, it was a Texas A&M home jersey. At Wembley. In London. In England.

Unfortunately, he was a fair way away and we were in a scrum to get on the underground, so walking over to him to deliver a high five would have been an ordeal. It cheered me up though, I felt warmer inside. The Steelers may have lost, but to my knowledge we outnumbered the Longhorns, 2-1. And I'll take any victory I can get.

During the Saturday on Texas A&M's bye week, it felt strange not walking to Kyle Field or staying up until 3:30 a.m. to watch A&M play a road game. After all, that had been my existence since the birth of the 2013 college football season.

Although I had reintegrated into British society, I was still noticing a number of cultural differences. For starters, I didn't need to carry water with me everywhere I went. On the topic of water, oh how I longed to buy 20 bottles from Walgreens for $2. That's cheap, you say? Yes, because the plastic bottles were faulty and couldn't stand up properly. I found this out the hard way.

Moreover, picking up phrases such as "howdy" and "y'all" had not aided me. I nonchalantly used these phrases when speaking to fellow Brits, and quickly acquired looks that suggested I'd just burned their house down. That's not all. Thanks to a Geico commercial that I was subjected to at least a thousand times on US television, I accidentally referred to Wednesday as "hump day." Needless to say, I was embarrassed on the same level as when I wore my dad's suit to my first-ever job interview.

Again, the use of language proved to rear its ugly head. Furthermore, it has always seemed a common bugbear of Brits that Americans call their number one sport—football. Their main argument is that compared to English football, you barely use your feet. That whole debate is as mind-numbingly boring as watching LeBron James or Clay Matthews star in yet another commercial. However, there are some American words that I failed to get on board with. The first—cleats. Cleats? I hadn't even heard of this word before. Why are they not called boots? The second example is uniforms. Again, surely these are kits?

Lastly, the phrase I failed to miss the most was an easy decision. It followed me everywhere I went, from being discussed on countless TV channels to dominating newspaper and internet headlines. Obamacare.

Perhaps my most crucial discovery explained why America is the leading superpower in the world. When I stumbled across it, I felt embarrassed that my fellow compatriots had dropped the ball in such a dramatic fashion.

Four words: six pack of beer.

In England, the normal pack size you'd usually find on a shelf is four. As a man that prides himself on being one ill-advised life choice away from alcoholism, I believe a four-pack simply isn't enough to satisfy. Because of this, I'm forced to buy two four-packs. Why is the six-pack so brilliant? The answer is simple. It's because it's the exact amount of beer that you need—a happy median. Four is too little and eight means you'll wake up the next morning to a world of regret.

So, with no Aggies in action, what was I going to do with my weekend? Eat fish and chips? Take in a game of soccer? Pop around to Buckingham Palace and see if the Queen fancies a game of croquet? Well, I did two out of the three.

On the Friday night, I was down in South West England in a little seaside town called Westward Ho. Why is this relevant? Because I came across a place that had exactly the same name a few miles from College Station. I know there are many towns and cities that share names between the UK and US, but this still seemed a bizarre coincidence. I wasn't going to shout about it, though. Once, my father went to Portsmouth in New Hampshire and proclaimed that he was from the original Portsmouth in Great Britain. They wholeheartedly did not care.

The next day, I headed to the place I'd spent most of my Saturdays from a scarily young age. Where? Fratton Park. The home of Portsmouth FC. Like Kyle Field is the Mecca to Aggies, Fratton is a spiritual home for me. It's where I originally fell in love with the sporting world.

Now, you're probably imagining this to be a park that is magical, sophisticated and a location where the best soccer in the land is played. Wrong, wrong and I wish.

To put it bluntly, Fratton Park is an eyesore from every angle. It's one of the last remaining old stadiums in England, and when I mean old, it was built in 1898. No, that is not a typo. 1898. In 2013, parts of the stadium had to be closed because of safety concerns. It's an absolute world away from Kyle Field or Reliant Stadium. To put it nicely, it's a complete dive. But it's home. And because of this, 15,000 people congregate every

Saturday to cheer on their forever-disappointing team. Why? Because they always have and always will.

It was my first homage of the season, and it hit home just how different the soccer and college football gameday experiences are. For the past two decades, had I ever thought of cooking some burgers in the parking lot behind the Fratton End? Had there ever been a march of honor? Did a World War II plane ever fly over? Of course not.

Whilst pondering further examples before kickoff, my afternoon suddenly took an inconvenient turn. As I tucked into a glorious sausage roll, a player who was warming up struck a ball in my general direction. As I was not looking, I had no idea what was about to happen. Splat. Straight in the face. It felt like I'd put my head through a red telephone box. My nose felt broken. I surveyed the area for sympathy. Nothing. Just people laughing at my horrible misfortune.

For the next ten minutes, I wasn't a happy bunny. Likewise, there was no marching band, Reveille or Kevin Sumlin saying, "Yes Sir," on the Jumbotron to cheer me up. Instead, there were more balls being kicked into the crowd. Was it wrong of me that I hoped someone else would get pelted so we could share and revel in the embarrassment together? Perhaps.

I took cover. It felt abnormal to experience a Saturday with no Aggie War Hymn, shouting "TOOOOOMBS" or getting hyped as I hear Kanye West's "Power" come on.

In its place, I was treated to a cheerful naval jingle and a big screen that looked like it may fall off its hinges at any moment and crush the people below. Luckily, that did not happen, although the screen did lose power on regular occasions.

That wasn't the only feature gaining my attention. Halfway through the second half, the opposition goalkeeper had a hot dog thrown at him because he was an ex-Southampton player. Comically, he had to complete the ninety-minutes with Heinz tomato ketchup dripping down the back of his jersey.

Maybe I had started to take the glitz and glamour of college football and the NFL for granted. On this day I was brought back down to earth with a thud. Literally. In the face.

16. International Spy Museum

S hortly before flying back to the US of A, I had dinner with some of my former co-workers. Their weary and drained faces further convinced me I was right to up sticks and set sail for Aggieland. When I asked if anything notable had happened since I left the company, my friend Dylan shrugged his shoulders and delivered the crushing words: "literally nothing."

My world seemed bigger now. Before, it was almost laughably small. Apart from my apartment, work, the pub, chippy, supermarket and Fratton Park, I never bothered venturing anywhere else.

I had often perceived the phrase "travel broadens the mind" to be a dreaded cliché that stood on par with "laughter is the best form of medicine." After all, if that was the case why aren't comedians replacing doctors?

Most people, including myself, travel to places that are solely committed to bringing in as much tourism as possible. Consequently, they end up losing their identity. Instead of broadening anything on my travels, all I really learned was that Diet Coke tastes differently on the other side of the world.

Texas had changed my outlook. This is a region that isn't renowned for people flying halfway across the world for a vacation. As a result, it has stayed true to itself. Although if you have little knowledge of the area, my advice is to refrain from booking a hotel in an area that has a nickname with the word "Guns" in it. To be fair to G-Town, as much as I didn't enjoy nearly being shot in the head or seeing a used blow-up sex doll in the hotel pool, at least it supplied me with a decent story to tell my mates down the pub. And with that in mind, maybe you shouldn't rule out staying there. After all, you do get a lovely view of an all-powerful highway interchange.

Before returning to Aggieland, I was set to fly into New York and stay for two nights before visiting my brother in Washington DC. From there I'd head to Pittsburgh for a short stopover and then on to Houston.

Whilst departing the plane, someone who worked at the airport greeted me.

"Bienvenidos a La Gran Manzana, señor!"

At first I thought he said, "Manziel." I was wearing a Texas A&M wristband and egotistically thought he may have been referring to it.

He proceeded to repeat the same sentence to each passenger that disembarked from the aircraft. Suddenly, I considered the likelihood of him preaching the ways of Johnny Football to be highly unlikely.

I assumed he was speaking Spanish, but I was unsure why. Had I just hopped on a plane to South America by mistake? It's not like I knew what he was saying. My knowledge of the Spanish language stretched to a few choice phrases, such as, "una cerveza por favor" (one beer please) and "dos cervezas por favor" (two beers please).

In the midst of my confusion, a large gutsy American finally responded to the eccentric gentleman.

"It's the big apple. We're in America. We speak English, you dumbass."

And that was that. I was back.

Even though I'd moonwalked through immigration without a hitch on the first leg of my adventure, I was still nervous about re-entering the country. Within seconds of handing my passport over, I was right to feel apprehensive. As I wasn't in employment, the immigration officer asked me some probing questions about how I planned to fund my second prolonged stay on these shores.

I surprised myself by remaining calm throughout. Following some further interrogation, I received the green light.

I woke up the next day wondering what to do with my Saturday. Go up the Empire State Building? Say hello to the Statue of Liberty? Get lost in Central Park?

None of the above. If I had learned anything in the Brazos Valley, it is that Saturdays should be spent doing one thing and one thing only. Watching college football.

Therefore, my first order of the day was to see what matchups there were. With A&M playing Ole Miss as late as 8:00 p.m. I had some time to kill.

Immediately, I noticed the Texas Longhorns were playing Oklahoma in one of the early games. That will do, I thought. Back in England, I support two soccer teams: Portsmouth and whomever Southampton is playing. This had spread to college football. I now found myself naturally rooting for UT's opposition.

The next item on the agenda was to find a place to watch it. NYC is abnormally large. I barely knew where to start. After Googling "college football bars in New York," I soon realized that there are dedicated watering holes for each college program across Manhattan.

Where better to support the Sooners than in an Oklahoma pub? I had visions of us locking arms, singing songs and celebrating the dramatic demise of the Longhorns' football dynasty.

Unfortunately, things didn't go to plan. I ended up sitting amongst hundreds of very miserable University of Oklahoma alumni. The initial cries of "boomer sooner" went mute. UT rolled them over. I could have reminded the Sooners about the 2012 Cotton Bowl, but I didn't fancy dislodging shards of glass from my skull.

Instead, I left as people drowned their sorrows. The next place on the agenda was the dedicated LSU bar for their mouthwatering SEC clash versus Florida. The atmosphere was much better, and it certainly helped that they were leading for the entire game. But it lacked any real meaning to me; I couldn't get into it. I headed back to my hotel during the third quarter. The large amounts of booze I'd consumed had caught up with me. A quick siesta before the A&M game seemed like a wise choice.

In hindsight, it wasn't. I felt like a sleepwalker as I rushed to Characters Bar & Grill—the home of the New York Aggies. With five minutes until kickoff, I was still ten blocks away.

When I walked in, a sense of pride engulfed me. The maroon shirts, the Texas accents and the pleasing yellow bottles of Shiner Bock. Even though I'm no Texan or Aggie in the literal sense, I felt like I was surrounded by my people. The experiences at the Sooners and LSU locations were fun, but it always appeared like something was missing. Here though, and as corny as it sounds, it felt right.

The Aggies took to the field at Vaught–Hemingway Stadium in an immaculate set of all-white uniforms. Meanwhile,

I was reminded of Bo Wallace's existence. I distinctly remembered the Ole Miss quarterback's performance against A&M in 2012. Back then, I thought he came across as someone that allegedly spends more time blow-drying his hair rather than studying a playbook. I suppose it's possible to do both at the same time, right?

Horror soon struck. Throughout the early stages of the game, Johnny Manziel went down injured and was clutching his knee. The whole place fell silent. You could have heard a pin drop. As Johnny winced, we collectively winced. All sorts of thoughts rushed through my mind. "Lord, take my knee instead!" "Anyone but Johnny!" and "I hope this place doesn't run out of booze!"

Johnny wasn't the only one I was feeling sorry for. A&M running back, Ben Malena, appeared to fumble the ball right next to the sideline. As ESPN panned to him standing on the edge of the field, he was wearing a headband that read "CASHOUT KING". The irony and embarrassment of such a king displaying a dodgy case of ball security resonated. Luckily, he was ruled to be out of bounds and the fumble was overturned. His blushes were spared.

When Manziel returned to the field, euphoric cheers filled the room. He was back and nothing was going to stop him.

Shortly after, an Aggie sitting in front of me asked if I knew who was wearing the number 17 jersey, because the player had no name on his back. However, he did have the name "Douglas" on display, so I was wondering if he was a new player that I hadn't heard of. I later discovered that Douglas was actually the name of the protective equipment that the Aggies wore. Luckily, I didn't put this forward as a suggestion, and claimed I didn't l know. Anyway, he detected my

English accent, told me his name was Mark and offered me a seat. I introduced myself and to my surprise, he asked if I was "...that English guy writing the book on A&M." Guilty. I embarrassingly felt like a Z-list celebrity.

He was there with his wife, Brittney; they typified why I felt comfortable around Aggies. Like I said, the LSU and Sooners bars were OK, but there simply wasn't that spirit or atmosphere that you get when you're surrounded by people from Aggieland. They lived near the A&M campus and like me, were in New York for the weekend. Just speaking to them for a few moments made me nostalgic for College Station. They were genuine, lovely people. As the game went on, we discussed everything from my time in Texas to the eleventh century castle that's located less than a mile away from where I lived back home.

We were soon joined by a couple of stragglers. One was an Aggie who was 78 years old and was in the class of '55. He was accompanied by his girlfriend, who at a guess, was in her mid-twenties. Well played, sir.

By this point, the game was strictly in the balance. Despite Mike Evans remarkably hurdling a defensive back, A&M trailed Ole Miss by seven points with not long left. For a brief moment I thought the Aggies would struggle to pull a rabbit out of the hat. Supporting the soccer team I do, you're naturally programmed to assume the worst—anything more than mediocrity is a delightful bonus. Halfway through the fourth quarter I was beginning to slip into autopilot and reach the conclusion that I'm a jinx on all of the sports teams I'm connected to.

Recklessly, I had not fully considered one component and the most important one of all: Johnny effin' Football.

The place erupted after a 4th and 7 gamble paid off. Everyone went bonkers. From then on there was only one man in the world you wanted in the driver's seat. With the help of a last-gasp, Josh Lambo field goal, A&M won 41-38.

The next day I woke up with a hangover the size of New Jersey. Not that I cared; the previous night was well worth the nauseating headaches that I had to valiantly fight off.

Moreover, I didn't have the luxury to wallow in my own filth. One of the crucial factors behind the desire to fly into New York was my Pittsburgh Steelers were playing the New York Jets on Sunday at MetLife Stadium. It was another chance to inhale more football, even though I felt like I could possibly hurl at any moment due to the previous night's Shiner Bock coming back to haunt me.

Regardless, I was due to meet a friend, Ashley, who I'd met at an NFL UK event a couple of months before. He had carried out the ingenious plan of whisking his wife away to New York whilst subtly sloping off to a football game as she hit the shops.

Once we had entered the future home of Super Bowl XLVIII, thankfully my hangover started to wear off. As a result, I plucked up the courage to get a round in. Within seconds, I almost fainted.

"Twenty-two dollars for two beers that aren't even pints?"

It's crazy how the NFL gets away with charging such ludicrous prices. Yes, I could boycott and refuse to pay, but when your team has a record of 0-4, you need as much pain relief as you can get. I begrudgingly handed over the cash.

Gratefully, my mind was taken off such daylight robbery as the Steelers finally turned up and rolled the Jets over to record their first 'W' of the season. What made the victory even sweeter was a Jets' fan had called me out for celebrating Geno Smith's second thrown interception of the afternoon. Usually, a bit of abuse is like water off a duck's back, I'm not bothered. Still, this cretin crossed the line.

Everyone that entered the stadium had been given a Breast Cancer Awareness ribbon. Naturally, I decided to display mine. The last thing I expected was a Jets' fan to call me a "Gaylord" because I was wearing a pink item. I bet his parents are extremely proud of him.

Throwing such blatant stupidity to one side, it was time to get ready to head to Washington DC.

During my time in the nation's capital, I seemed to be a walking conversation starter.

On one particular occasion, I was stood in the queue for the International Spy Museum when a security guard shouted at me. Apparently, if you wear the maroon and white of Texas A&M, it is a free invitation for a Washingtonian to shout the words: "Johnny Football" at you.

This wasn't an isolated incident. After the eighth or ninth time, it began to wear a little thin. It was pleasant at first. I'd give a nice smile; maybe even throw in a thumbs-up if I was feeling bold.

Don't get me wrong; I thought it was neat that Johnny had put A&M into the forefront of mainstream culture. It was merely a shock from being in Aggieland where nine out of ten people wear maroon clobber on a daily basis. Never had anyone shouted at me down there for my choice of threads—just my mode of transport!

Anyway, my time on the East Coast wasn't solely spent having to awkwardly deal with strangers bellowing at me. It had its other perks, too. Well, one very good one actually. My greatest American sporting achievement.

Back home it's a well-known fact I have a dusty bookcase that's almost half full of soccer trophies, accolades and other generic stuff made from fake silver.

David Beckham once described me as the footballer he looked up to as a child. OK, it may not have been the real "Becks," but he was a kid that was a couple of grades below me at school. He may have also technically been named Darren Beachum.

The relevance? Well, when it came to traditional American sports, I had nothing to show for. Essentially, I was invisible in the US sporting hierarchy. A ghost. Until a fateful day in October.

I was at a professional ice hockey match merely going about my business. Drink in one hand; foam finger on the other, when something curious happened. An announcement was made. Out of the blue, everyone perked up. They sensed we could be on the brink of a special occasion. Oh my, how right they were.

"IF A GOAL IS SCORED IN THE NEXT TWO MINUTES, EVERYONE IN ATTENDANCE WILL WIN A BIG MAC FROM MCDONALDS."

This was it. The pinnacle. Surely, it would put me on the map? I'd no longer be unseen in the US sporting world. Perhaps ESPN may run with it? I settled with the conclusion that I'd at least be a talking point between Skip Bayless and Stephen A Smith on *First Take*. Before all of that hullabaloo though, someone had to score.

With seconds remaining in the allocated win-a-Big Mac timeframe, finally. A goal. The drink went one way. The foam finger, the other. Jubilation. Elation. Triumph.

I'd done it. I'd won McDonalds' greatest ever creation. You simply can't put a price on such a victory. (OK maybe $2, or whatever a Big Mac is worth). But this was my time. Other people run marathons, swim great lakes or win little league baseball tournaments; I sit there and wait for multi-millionaire hockey players to score a goal so I can win a Big Mac. We're all good at different things. And even more beautifully, I now had something else to add to my dusty bookcase that cherishes my many sporting accomplishments. The crème de la crème of greatness. A crusty and moldy hamburger.

My next stop was Pittsburgh, Pennsylvania. As much as I was excited to return to Texas, I was equally eager to revisit the place that led me to falling in love with football. On my travels I learned that Pittsburgh does not contain a particularly exotic reputation. For me, I loved everything about it. My trips to see my parents were always memorable. I'd return home fifty pounds heavier and with a suitcase so full of Steelers' gear that I'd struggle to explain my cargo to customs.

The night before I was due to fly to Houston, I stayed at a hotel that was slap bang next to Pittsburgh Airport. Airport hotels are like no other. I could say with a high degree of certainty that I don't think anyone has ever stayed in one for more than a solitary night. The turnover of people must be mind bending. At this particular hotel they were barely interested in my name. All they wanted to know was my flight time and number.

Equally, it became apparent that the hotel workers lived in the hotel. It was a seemingly strange setup. Did they ever leave? It confused me in the same way that tollbooth operators do. Who are these people? Where do they come from? And the crucial question that really peaks my interest: Where do they park their cars? It's universally understood that you never see a parking lot near a tollbooth.

With such earth-shattering questions spinning through my mind, it's a miracle I ended up back in the Brazos Valley without a bump in the road. However, I'd soon be nursing a significant migraine, as Texas A&M had just lost 45-41 to SEC rivals, Auburn.

As the game finished, I sat there for six hours, motionless and distraught. (OK, it was probably only a few minutes or seconds, but it felt like a lifetime). No one had seen this defeat coming. In the corresponding fixture in 2012, A&M romped to a 63-21 victory.

All I wanted to do was go to Denny's, order half the menu and eat/cry myself to sleep. I didn't though, because that would be a bit weird, tragic and also pretty expensive.

Instead, I ate steak fajitas in a dark Mexican eatery. Probably a close second in the tragedy rankings behind a visit to Denny's. I insisted that all sharp objects should be kept at an arm's length.

It turned out to be the perfect place to reflect. At this juncture I was happy to admit that I'd developed an almost unhealthy obsession with a certain chap called Johnny Manziel. I seriously counted myself lucky that I got to watch this guy play.

We may never see someone like Johnny in college football again, let alone in maroon and white. Seeing his reaction to the defeat hit me the hardest. The game was a rollercoaster of emotions. One minute, Aggies everywhere were partying like it was a wedding. The next, Kyle Field descended into a funeral.

The undoubted turning point was the first play of the fourth quarter. With every receiver covered, Johnny scrambled outside of the pocket and was crunched by an inside linebacker. His throwing arm had been obliterated. Unsurprisingly, this forced him to leave the field to be checked out by a horde of medical staff. Despite A&M leading at the time of his injury, the defense simply couldn't contain Auburn. With the game slipping away, Manziel re-entered the field and nearly won the game in the dying moments even though he was effectively throwing with an arm that had been sat on by an enormous 300 lb. dude. I can tell you from experience that hurts. And no, I'm not willing to disclose the details of how it happened to me. Some things are best left unsaid. After Johnny's never-say-die heroics, all the so-called experts that questioned his leadership, motivation and attitude could now quite frankly, sit down and shut up.

Away from the serious stuff, other aspects came to light in my hours of vague Samuel Adams Oktoberfest induced thoughts. Firstly, I didn't like the style of Aggies' backup quarterback, Matt Joeckel's helmet.

Secondly, I harbored a feeble hatred for Auburn's head coach Gus Malzahn, and I didn't really know why. Perhaps it was because he didn't wear his visor with anywhere near as much swag as Kevin Sumlin did. Even before A&M played Auburn, I'd seen Malzahn on TV and thought he came across as the type of guy that would possibly charge onto the field of his son's high school soccer practice and head-butt the referee for no apparent reason. In reality, I'm sure he is a lovely, dignified chap.

Thirdly, after a controversial and blatant miss from the referee late in the game, I never wanted to hear the phrase "horse collar," ever again. Other than that, the usual bile filled my brain such as the realization that Hank Schrader from *Breaking Bad* looks like an overweight Bruce Willis.

Furthermore, I pondered an attention-grabbing observation that I'd cooked up whilst attending both NFL and NHL games in recent weeks. At a sporting event you can be seated next to a human that seems personable, genuine and more importantly, doesn't make a fuss when you exit the row to go and take a leak. Likewise, they will share some insightful and charming opinions on the game. Before you get the opportunity to ask this hero if he'd like to be best man at your future unplanned wedding... BAM.

A t-shirt or sandwich is cannoned into the crowd by some organization, such as Chick-fil-A or Subway. Deep down, everyone knows they've just witnessed a game changer. The mask and gloves come off. Carnage. All out war. It's everyone for themselves.

I had to dodge at least six elbows at the Verizon Center as people clambered for a showering of free sandwiches. The guy next to me got a hand to one, but fumbled it. A man sitting to his immediate right recovered it. Both his feet were down. It was a fair catch. No penalty flag needed to be thrown.

The dude that controversially missed out on the chicken goodness couldn't let it go. Before that outburst of anarchy, he cut a harmonious and amicable figure. Now, he was seething. As the interceptor devoured his sandwich, the whole aisle received a potent whiff of the white meat. It didn't help proceedings. I sensed the fuming protagonist burning up inside. Meanwhile, I was basking in the lunacy of it all.

That story helped put the defeat to Auburn into perspective. Yes, I was devastated that A&M had lost. But at the end of it all, my day wasn't ruined by the fact I had missed out on a chicken sandwich. And I, for one, take great solace in that.

In hindsight, the defeat to Auburn shouldn't have been as crushing as it was. Eleven weeks later they would be ranked #2 in the country and play Florida State in the BCS National Championship Game. Unfortunately for my good pal Gus, they lost in the last minute, 34-31.

Regardless, it was time for A&M to set their sights on another SEC rival in the form of Vanderbilt Commodores.

Question: Have you ever gone to a liquor store and asked the person behind the counter if they have any minty-fresh flavored beer? No? Well done; you're not an irrational mentalist. And if you have, you are probably the one individual that loves 11:21 a.m. kickoff times.

There aren't many things in this world that anger me. However, my alcoholic beverages being ruined due to someone deciding that the college football game I'm attending should kickoff ridiculously early in the morning is something that does.

After brushing my gnashers shortly before tailgating, I failed to shrug the "toothpastey" taste from my palate. Miller Lite had rapidly transformed into Mint Lite. Eventually, I got over this faux pas and moved on with my life. The day before I'd been given perspective—I almost didn't have a life to move on with.

I know what you're thinking. Crazy driver? Heat exhaustion? Heart attack from eating another Lumberjack Slam? Nope. Golf ball.

Up until this point, in all my time in Aggieland, I'd never seen a soul on the university campus golf course. This soon changed in the form of a rude awakening.

My ordeal began when I was walking down George Bush Drive. I was merely going about my business whilst pondering why Aggieland didn't have a Dunkin Donuts. After all, I'd been led to believe that "America runs on Dunkin." College Station seemed like it was doing reasonably fine without one.

Before I had the opportunity to dwell on alleged broken advertising laws for a second longer, I heard the elegant sound of a golf ball dropping onto freshly cut grass. A golfer had delightfully approached the green with a gracefully timed chip shot. I stopped to admire the glory of it. I started clapping and ironically called out in my best American accent, "In the hole!" Everyone was having a lovely time. Well, until he four-putted on the green. Things turned sour. He hadn't done himself, or his on-looking family of five, justice.

I continued walking. The greenery and the smell of a fresh October day filled the air. That's when out of nowhere, a golf ball came trickling down the sidewalk at literally four or five miles an hour. It was coming right for me. I'll be honest, I was terrified. Who wouldn't be?

With this precarious position unfolding, I speedily transformed into Jack Bauer from the TV show, 24. If I refused to negotiate with terrorists, I certainly wasn't about to start negotiating with oncoming golf balls.

So what did I do? I nonchalantly let the ball zoom between my legs. I don't like to write my own reviews, but I must say the way I ignored the pending ball of doom would have made any female within a hundred yards swoon. Shortly afterwards, reality struck. A large gentleman came waddling in my direction. He wanted to know where his ball ended up. I delivered the crushing news that it had probably made its way to South Texas Avenue by that point, and it was probably best he took a drop shot. He was incensed. Oh well, it served him right for nearly dismantling one of my ankles.

Vanderbilt marked the sixth home game of the season. After sleepily meandering in the general direction of my tailgate and yawning at least seven hundred times, I was ready to roll.

On my journey I observed some slick tailgating traditions. Firstly, the "throw something onto a wooden board game." I'm not quite sure what it was, but it encapsulated my imagination. In the space of 200 yards, I saw this game being played at least a dozen times. In a society where the Xbox and PlayStation rule the roost, I was relatively impressed that these old-fashioned games still occurred. Or perhaps because it was so early in the day, people's eyes couldn't take the strain of playing Madden or Call of Duty on widescreen. Who knows?

In the build up to the game, there were murmurs that Johnny Manziel wasn't going to be fit enough to play. After busting his shoulder against Auburn, there had been numerous sightings of the Aggies quarterback wearing a sling around the university campus. Fortunately, with kickoff drawing closer and closer, news leaked out that Johnny had been named as the official starter.

As I entered Kyle Field, I knew I was going to be seated in roughly the same spot as I was for the Alabama game. Once again I'd be amongst the enemy. In truth, I relished the opportunity. Also, I liked how the away teams' fans were spread out in all four corners of Kyle Field. It certainly helps to nullify their impact and enforce the 12th Man into everyone's senses.

Luckily for me, Vandy's band didn't travel. God bless that verdict. Then again, after a few minutes I'd reached the conclusion that perhaps a marching band would have drowned out some of the bile that I had to endure.

Within the first quarter a portly chap bellowed, "If you can't get into Texas, you go to A&M!"

I swiftly retorted that, "If you can't get into A&M, you go to Vanderbilt." He muffled some academic statistics at me, but right on time Derel Walker caught an eight-yard pass from Johnny to record A&M's first touchdown of the morning. I no longer heard him, as the 12th Man ringed out. He never repeated that chant again. I had won the battle, but had I won the war?

Well, yes. All they brought to the table were a batch of pom-poms on sticks. Terrifying. Interestingly, I later got one joisted into my back. Was it intentional? I guess I'll never know. I shrugged it off and continued to wave my towel to restrict their view.

In the wake of that, I didn't hear a peep for the rest of the game. Although just before, a Vandy supporter had audibly enquired if the Aggies were sponsored by ATM machines because of the university logo. I couldn't help but laugh. It was the single worst piece of trash talking I'd ever heard. You could sense that after the words left his mouth, even he was ashamed. D-. Must do better, son.

Sadly for that sorrowful individual, Trey Williams showed he's clearly a morning person as he registered an average of 10.8 yards per carry. In addition, Vandy's misery was compounded by the brilliance of Malcome Kennedy who was extremely unlucky not to add a touchdown to his 83 receiving yards. His chums, LaQuvionte Gonzalez and Derel Walker did snare three between them though.

During the third quarter the Aggies completed an unwanted trio of fumbles. On this subject, it always amazed me how slow football players were to recover fumbles. The moment I drop food, I scoop it up within a millisecond.

Before I knew it, the game brought about something I'd never seen before. A pooch punt. I'm still not entirely sure why the Commodores did it or even what one actually is, but it was hilarious. The quarterback ballooned the ball up into the air for pretty much no reason. Well, as far as I could tell anyway. It didn't seem to give them any advantage. It gave us all a good laugh, though.

It took large cojones. It reminded me of when at a restaurant a waiter comes around with a plate of food that you haven't ordered and asks if you did. Ninety-nine people out of 100 politely say no. But there is always one who will push the boundaries. On this occasion it was Vanderbilt's maverick offensive coordinator.

In spite of this, A&M won the game 56-24, and suddenly everything in the world seemed holy again.

However, later that night I wasn't celebrating much.

I'd nipped out for a bottle of water at a local gas station when something peculiar happened. Two men hurtled past me. They were running for their lives. The gust of wind from their slipstream almost toppled me over. I soon realized why. Five seconds later, the heavens opened. It was like someone had turned a hose on and jetted it in my direction.

Worse was still to come. I heard thunder rumbling in the distance.

I weaved through puddles and what I perceived to be forked lightning like a less muscular Trey Williams.

Eventually, I got to safety. Yes, I may have been soaking wet, but A&M had won and I wasn't as depressed as I was the Saturday before, and that my friends is considered as a success.

17. All Hallows' Eve

Whilst munching on my eighth mouthful of Manchu Wok's underrated General Tso's chicken, I couldn't help but observe some notable differences about Post Oak Mall. No, a dog had not escaped from The Puppy Station.

For a moment I wasn't able to quite put my finger on it. Then it hit me. The vast amount of spider's webs and fake skeletons could only mean one thing. I'd soon get my first taste of Halloween, American style.

Yanks take this yearly event to a whole different level compared to us Brits and well, everyone else in the world. Back home if you had the balls to knock on someone's door and demand candy, you'd be applauded for your audacity. Why? Because it's more than likely the police would be called, or you'd be abducted.

As yet, the Halloween culture hasn't properly infiltrated British shores. It's primarily seen as something our transatlantic cousins go crazy for. Yes, there are fancy dress parties for students and the odd, isolated, upper-class neighborhood will stage an unconventional "trick or treating" scene, but it's certainly a minority.

Instead, we go nuts for a holiday that takes place just a few days later. Strap yourself in folks, here comes a history lesson.

November 5th—Guy Fawkes Night.

Back in 1605, a cheeky chappy called Guy Fawkes was part of a gunpowder plot. He was guarding explosives that were designed to blow up the Houses of Parliament and the King of England. The plot failed and as a result, this night represents the significance. Families with children as young as four or five create effigies of Guy Fawkes and burn them on a bonfire.

Following that, hundreds of fireworks are set off. It's pretty cool, but you usually end up almost freezing to death because of the baltic November temperatures.

This was the first year in living memory that I wouldn't be attending a Guy Fawkes Night. Halloween was under pressure to deliver.

Naturally, my first port of call was a visit to a fancy dress shop. To my surprise, this place didn't sell the usual selection of Superman or Ghostbusters outfits. Oh no. I was heavily traumatized by what I saw lingering in the depths of the store. In every direction there was something horrific. As well as boxes of sawn-off rubber fingers, you had the ability to buy statues of demented children. And if that didn't whet your appetite, the option to purchase a zombie being electrocuted in a rocking chair was listed at half price.

So, what costume would I go for? Originally, I wanted to go as Kenny Powers from Eastbound and Down. Frustratingly, this store only seemed to sell costumes with bloody and deformed limbs hanging off them. This left me with no other option than to turn up at Northgate as an English football hooligan. It's the perfect fancy dress outfit, because it requires minimal effort. All I had to do was wear an England jersey, throw a metal chair through a glass window and end up getting arrested. Even I could manage that.

The early stages of October 31st were enthralling. I walked around the campus and saw approximately nine Scooby Do's. At first I thought a shop must be heavily discounting these outfits, but soon realized Scooby Do was what Johnny Manziel had personified during 2012's festivities. I couldn't help but wonder what Reveille thought of all these human dogs trying to invade her territory. As well as these six-foot canines bounding around, the hundreds of pumpkins that I was seeing everywhere intrigued me. For the record, I'm not entirely sure whether a pumpkin is a fruit or vegetable. We don't see many in England. Well we may, but I've never considered anything orange, especially burnt orange, to be particularly pleasant, so it's likely if they are in English supermarkets, I choose to ignore them.

On my way back from the campus, I was really looking forward to the night's festivities. My brother from another mother, Zach, had invited me over to his place for pregame drinks before hitting Northgate.

Unfortunately, my excitement was short lived. Some impulsive teenagers that were probably buzzing from too much Halloween candy decided to slow their car down and bark in my direction. I had my headphones in so I couldn't decipher what they were preaching. By the time I reacted they'd already sped off into the distance. It was probably the twentieth time this had happened, so I laughed it off and quickly forgot about it.

It's fair to say I wasn't in a similar forgiving mood when about a mile down the road, the exact same car started crawling alongside me again. I barely believed that they'd undertaken a U-turn all in the pathetic attempt to goad an oblivious pedestrian. This time I heard exactly what they were saying.

"Hey walker! Are you so poor that you can't afford a car?"

They then gestured by wiping their eyes. In all honesty, I was astonished by the whole episode.

"Wah! Wah! Are you heading home to cry, you loser?"

Before this disruptive character finished his sentence, a wry smile adorned my face. Why? Because they'd just been stopped by a set of traffic lights. For the next minute or so, I had an opportunity to respond.

Whilst approaching the car, it was clear that the protagonist was beginning to get twitchy.

"Sorry mate, I may have misheard, but it seemed like you had a couple of opinions that you'd like to share with me."

Immediately, he slouched back into his seat. His accomplices were red with embarrassment. He couldn't muster a single word.

"Yes. That's what I thought. Anyway, I'd rather walk than drive around in your heap of junk. I've seen better looking lawn mowers."

The lights went green. They drove off with their tails between their legs.

Once I got back to my travel tavern, I considered if I'd been a little harsh to the scoundrels in the car. I quickly snapped out of such madness. To be fair, I had ignored their first outcries; it was the fact they bizarrely came back for another bite at the cherry that hacked me off. Oh well, I was sure they wouldn't be shouting at pedestrians anytime soon. Before I reflected on it further, Zach and his girlfriend, Amy, had picked me up.

After washing down some naughty shots of Jägermeister with copious amounts of beer, we turned up at a nearby house party. The first thing that struck me was how nice the student digs were. These houses were immaculately furnished. Compared to my student housing back in the good ol' days, I was understandably envious.

A few days before, I had wandered past some fraternity and sorority houses. These took my breath away. They were lofty mansions with sports cars parked outside. I couldn't help but compare my university experience with theirs—I highly doubted they had ever eaten cold kebabs out of wrinkly newspapers, used a shower curtain as a form of bedding or utilized Yellowbook's as toilet rolls.

In my third year, the house I abided in was literally falling apart. On two separate occasions, I walked through the front door and noticed that the kitchen roof had fallen through. That was nothing. The walls were riddled with damp, the windows were cracked and we regularly had a homeless man called Jimbo sleeping in our front garden. The weird stains on the carpet and the unique lingering smell barely registered because the place was such a foul dump. To top things off, there was a locked World War II bunker at the bottom of our garden. We were convinced it housed dead bodies—it would have certainly explained the odd stench.

Soon enough, we moved onto a second party. Following a solid ten minutes whereby my accent was playfully ridiculed, I was starting to feel the effects of the alcohol I'd swigged all evening.

Regardless, the only option was to power through. A big night lay ahead. Whilst holding that thought, a cop turned up at the front door. He asked us to turn the music down and make less noise. I felt a little underwhelmed. As I was dressed like a football hooligan, I was more than prepared for the place to be stormed by riot police. Unfortunately, my visions of having an ironic scrap evaporated.

To my horror, Zach had locked up. We were now waiting for our lift to arrive. After drinking a considerable amount of fluids, I was in agony. I wouldn't be able to hold on until we got to Northgate. Funnily enough, I didn't fancy pissing myself on the way there. Plus, I had previous. Three years earlier on the way to a soccer game, I was sinking pints like never before. I was a man possessed. On the underground I felt like I was on the brink. Even though the next stop wasn't the one we were due to exit, I hopped off and inelegantly ran to the nearest bush to offload.

Wonderfully, this time I wasn't alone. Zach's housemate, Gage, was in a similar position. Before I knew it, I had turned around to see Gage, who was dressed as a six-foot penguin, relieving himself into a pot plant situated in a random house's front garden. The lunacy of it made me start to uncontrollably laugh. This increased the pressure on my bladder.

Within a minute, I was re-enacting Gage's get-out clause. I couldn't help but think if the people that lived in the house had opened their curtains they'd have received an exclusive teaser to the future motion picture, *The Full Monty 2: Penguin and Hooligan Let it All Hang Out*. In all honesty, I was so plastered I wouldn't have cared. In my delirious mind I was doing them a favor by watering their dying greenery.

Figuratively speaking, I was off my tits. The scary thing was, we hadn't even made it to the promised land of Northgate yet.

We soon would, though. The landscape was filled with countless people dressed as Miley Cyrus and Scooby Do. I'd never seen so many scantily clad women in my life. The following Saturday, the second I told my tailgating pal, Chris

Barnard, that I'd been to Northgate for Halloween, he responded, "How was I hate my daddy night?"

The district was swarming with people. When we finally entered somewhere, we had to be careful not to trample over people that had already passed out. At the bar when ordering a round, I had to hand over seven IDs. I could safely say I'd never done that before. Back home, as long as you're waving some legal tender around and you're tall enough to peer over the bar, you will get served with a smile.

With a pint in hand, a stranger shouted in my direction. He was a fellow Brit that was a student at A&M, and had clocked my jersey. After going over and drunkenly giving him an ironic hug, it quickly became apparent that despite his garbled outcry, he wasn't best pleased to see me.

As well as claiming to dislike people from the South of England, he declared he was tired of people first hearing his accent and then asking if he was, "that English dude writing the book." I apologized for the inconvenience and realized that the hug was probably misplaced.

In his defense, apart from the blatant prejudice towards Southerners and other people's innocent presumptions, I kind of understood why he had given me a frosty reception. As soon as I got to Aggieland, people were automatically giving me names and contact details of other Brits. What they failed to realize was that I'd just traveled thousands of miles to get away from these people, so why would I want to be surrounded by them here? I didn't bother dwelling on the sorry state of Britain's abnormal socializing methods for much longer. I had far more important things to do, like downing another sake bomb.

The next morning, I woke up with a fez on my head and half an uneaten Whataburger meal next to me. No, that is not a euphemism. Where had I retrieved the fez? I vaguely remembered finding it on the sidewalk next to a gas station and wearing it for the rest of the night. Clearly, it wasn't my first rodeo.

As my brain swirled in agony, there was an ominous knock at the door. It was Clay Taylor and Andrew Cagle from TexAgs. They had turned up to film a promotional feature about my time in Aggieland.

Once they'd set up the camera, I was feeling nauseous. The worst aspect was that I could barely string two words together. My brain was struggling to generate simple words and phrases. Not only that, I was as white as a drained, pale bed sheet. Quite simply, I was a mess. Northgate had destroyed me—again.

When they departed I felt guilty and sensed I'd let them down. They had turned up hoping to get me in top form, and instead I was nothing more than a decaying vegetable.

Luckily, after Clay and Andrew weaved their magic on the piece, it came out better than I could have ever imagined. Considering what they had to work with, it was a real testament to their incredible talents.

I went straight back to bed. I convinced myself that the only way I was going to get over this dreadful hangover was by sleeping it off. Awkwardly, this came with some noticeable drawbacks.

By this point in my stay, I was suffering from a heavy bout of cabin fever. The four walls were beginning to close in on me. Not only that, but I realized my situation was getting bleak the minute I found myself striking up a friendship with a lingering fly. His name was Kevin.

If you think that's bad, during one afternoon I refused to live through the droning sound of the air conditioning unit any longer that I resorted to an afternoon in Chuck E. Cheese's. No grown man should ever have to admit to that. It was equally humiliating as it was glorious, with a victory over a moody teenager at basketball free throws proving to be the biggest highlight. It was an achievement that ranked on par with winning the hot potato game on three consecutive occasions when I was five years old. The perfect hat-trick.

So, there I was, trying my hardest to sleep off this monstrous headache. Regrettably, my next-door neighbor had other ideas. Like clockwork there was large banging against the paper-thin wall at regular intervals throughout the day. This wouldn't be a couple of knocks here and there. It was non-stop. Judging by the noises that accompanied the headboard's battering, it didn't require a genius to work out that a hooker was occupying the room next to mine. At one point, with the partition shaking with such verve, I half expected the hanky panky participants to burst through into my room at any moment. Because I had usually been out during the day, I rarely took in the travel tavern's surroundings in sunlight. I soon realized why.

The nights weren't much better. A few days before Hookergate, I woke up to someone trying to knock my door down. Naturally, I was bricking it. What on earth was happening? There was no way I was going to open the door. I kept my cool and looked through the peephole. I saw an idiot that was so legless he thought my room was his. Even more worryingly, I could only see his top half and he was naked. I didn't want to know any more details. I slumped back to bed and tried to convince myself it was all just an inconvenient dream.

All of these anecdotes barely scratch the surface compared to Marge. Who's Marge? She is a hoarder that lived, and probably still lives, on the bottom floor of the travel tavern. My room was directly above hers, so whenever I walked down the stairs I always strolled past her window. Without trying to invade her privacy, I never looked through the glass at first. It was only until the third or fourth time that I noticed in my peripheral vision something about her room was heavily out of sync. The next time, my curiosity got the better of me and I caught a peek. Mountains of junk, pizza boxes and general trash dominated the room. I was perplexed. After gaining a second opinion through Clay and Andrew, her hoarder status was confirmed. Later on, we affectionately named her, Marge. It suited her. Classic Marge.

Following a day of little sleep and feeling like my stomach had the capability to implode at any moment, I chose to remove myself from my bed and head for midnight yell.

On my way to Kyle Field, I felt every ounce of energy being sapped from my body. I had a dilemma. Although my tummy was in pieces, not eating all day had caught up with me.

When you're hungry you make rash and foolish decisions. Before I knew it, I was sat in Double Dave's devouring as much pizza and pepperoni rolls as I could wrap my mucky digits around.

The consequences were nothing short of disastrous. As I walked into the direction of Kyle Field's blazing and glittery floodlights, I sensed something wasn't quite right. The sounds coming from my midriff were not human. Throw in some fairly painful abdominal cramps and I quickly found myself proficiently jogging along George Bush Drive, hoping and praying I wasn't about to commit an unholy act on the side of the road.

Fortunately, I managed to hold on. However, my torment was far from over. Once I arrived at the stadium, it's fair to say I'd never been so happy to see a portable toilet in all of my life—in no uncertain terms, I was turtle necking.

Oh, the shame. Sitting in complete darkness whilst half of your insides flop out the bottom of you doesn't exactly fill you with much pride. A small tear exited the corner of my bloodshot eye.

Despite this, I tried to remain defiant. Things could have been a lot worse. How? Firstly, I might have been caught short. Secondly, I thanked my lucky stars there was toilet paper located by my side. Thirdly, this whole episode reminded me of a musical festival that I attended in 2009. A group of lads were on a stag do (bachelor party) and what I witnessed has stayed with me ever since. Over the years, British stag do's have evolved into crazy, outrageous and wild events that can often last as long as a couple of weeks. For instance, some of these do's can involve bizarre shenanigans such as the stag getting handcuffed to a train of naked dwarfs.

If you think that's bad, it was moderately tame compared to what I saw at V Festival. Whilst the groom-to-be was in a portable toilet, his so-called friends decided to shake the structure he was occupying. Seconds later, the situation drastically escalated. Now, the portable toilet had been turned over onto its side. Without a second thought, this baying mob started to roll the structure down a hill. Once it hit the bottom, the door flung open. The stag stepped out and was covered head to toe in used toilet roll, dirty diapers and other people's bodily waste.

With that truly horrifying image in your head, I'll attempt to swing the focus to football. The following day, Texas A&M played the penultimate game of my trip against UTEP Miners.

Speaking bluntly, the game wasn't particularly alluring. At times it felt like we were watching men against boys as the Aggies ran out 57-7 winners. To put that into context, zero points were scored in the fourth quarter. As the game was won by half time, Coach Sumlin clearly decided against running up the score. To be honest, A&M could have quite easily reached treble figures. This was another mini learning curve for me. In US sports in general, it is seen as derogatory and heavily disrespectful to keep piling points on the board. Back in the UK, sportsmanship goes out of the window. With aspects like goal difference playing a big part in overall standings, everyone wants to inflict as much heartache on the opposition's players and fans as possible.

With the Aggies decked out in a stylish all-Maroon number, standout performers included running backs Ben Malena and Brandon Williams. Both ran UTEP ragged and accumulated 144 yards between them. In terms of receiving, Mike Evans was given a sun lounger for the afternoon after racking up 364 yards and 6 touchdowns during the two previous weekends. Travis Labhart carried the torch and put in an effective display that saw him record two touchdowns and 83 receiving yards.

Regardless of the straightforward matchup, there were some visible aspects that stood out. A majority of people were dressed in coats, jumpers, gloves and woolly hats. I was taken aback. It wasn't cold in the slightest. It was mild compared to the British Isles! Late in the game, A&M running back Tra Carson went down with a suspected neck injury. I'd never heard an environment descend into such silence. The only noise you heard was the student section stepping off the metal girders. Thankfully, Tra would end up being fine.

Lastly, throughout the game, I couldn't help but notice that an excessive amount of spider webs were floating through the air. Comically, the man behind me cooked up a rumor and claimed it was actually whales' semen. How he even came up with such an idea I'd rather not know. Nonetheless, an alarming amount of people fell for it. Once I'd got back to my travel tavern, I learned the spider webs were part of a process that is known as ballooning. It is when young spiders emerge and disperse strands of silk from their abdomens. Apparently, it regularly happens in Texas during the fall.

Again, it went to show that every day was a school day in Aggieland. Plus, I was thankful it wasn't semen.

18. The T Word

When I first arrived at Texas A&M, I was only aware of a handful of the university's core traditions. During my stay I promptly discovered and experienced a majority of these time-honored practices.

As I entered my final week in Aggieland, I couldn't help but reflect on all of the traditions that I had the immense pleasure of sampling.

Midnight Yell Practice: It still gives me goosebumps when I look back to my first full day in College Station. I was feeling a little sorry for myself and started to think that perhaps my whole adventure was born out of complete lunacy. However, witnessing yell practice gave me the belief I was doing the right thing. Just seeing all those people pouring into a heavily lit Kyle Field was truly special. Even though I nearly had a heart attack when I first heard the cannon, I was mesmerized throughout. It sounds extremely corny, but it was the first indication that I was going to fall in love with Aggieland.

The 12th Man: It was an almighty honor to stand with the 12th Man. Kyle Field's east side is often described as the best student section in college football, and from what I saw and experienced I'd certainly endorse that statement.

The Seattle Seahawks may try and claim the title with their cheesy attempts at trying to be the loudest fans in the world, but they'll never be the original 12th Man, and they'll never be able to replicate the unique and one-off atmosphere of Kyle Field.

One of my favorite moments of my entire trip was seeing 12th Man walk on, Sam Moeller, block a punt against Mississippi State. It single-handily typified the tradition, and proved why it's so special and unique.

The Fightin' Texas Aggie Band: Out of all the Aggie traditions the band surprised me the most. I have the musical ability of a box of cereal. As a result, I didn't expect to enjoy the band as much as I did. To this day it blows my mind how they manage to put the choreography together without some poor soul falling into a sousaphone or tuba. Before I saw them in action, I didn't think the combination of sports and music was a good one. With their brilliance they managed to turn that opinion on its head. I soon found myself looking forward to halftime so I'd get to see them in action. Also, a quick shout out to the chap that introduces them at the north end of Kyle Field; his voice is legendary.

Yell Leaders: I'll be honest; I had no idea who these dudes were at first. I was baffled as I watched them carry out their mini dance routines and then start running up and down the touchline. It didn't take long for everything to make perfect sense. They play a massive part in preserving the atmosphere and relaying yells to the 12th Man. If I was a student at A&M and didn't have a hope of becoming the football team's punter, would I want to be a yell leader? You bet your arse I would. Unfortunately, due to the heat and the fact I'd struggle to remember all the routines, I'd probably be laughed out of the place.

Reveille: Shortly after arriving in Aggieland, whilst standing in a queue at Fuego Tortilla Grill, I couldn't help but overhear a couple of students angrily discussing the topic of someone called "Reveille" not receiving a military funeral. At first I thought this was perhaps a former student that had tragically perished in the Middle East. It wasn't until the same subject came up again later in the day that I asked someone who Reveille was. Their face suggested that I should be deported from Aggieland immediately.

Gig 'em: This saying always takes me back to the initial stages of planning my trip to Texas when I read an article that said you'll be fine in College Station as long as you put your thumb up and say "gig 'em" on regular occasions. Unsurprisingly, I followed this advice. I was fascinated to hear that this gesture originated from a 1930 yell practice before A&M played TCU. A man named Pinky Downs shouted, "What are we going to do to those Horned Frogs?" and followed it up with "Gig 'em, Aggies!" while raising his thumb. It wasn't until I learned that a gig is a spear-like tool used for frog hunting that I fully understood the saying. I bloody love it, though.

The Aggie Ring: On my first journey to Kyle Field, the last thing I expected to come across was a 12-foot, 6,500-pound ring. It was enormous. I soon noticed a majority of Aggies strolling around and wearing their own versions of this form of jewelry with immense pride. My friend, Chris Barnard, let me try on his for a couple of moments; I sensed how much the ring meant to him. It summed up the connection that Texas A&M has with its current and former students. If I had a ring that represented my university back in England, would I wear it? Not a chance. Why? Because in the three years that I attended, I never felt a connection or bond to the place. Aggies are different; they love shouting from the rooftops about their lifetime attachment to their university, and I understood why.

Bonfire: I had read about the Aggie Bonfire tragedy before arriving in Texas. In 1999, the Bonfire fell taking the lives of 12 people and injuring 27 others. As well as remembering the lives that were lost, the Bonfire Memorial stands as a celebration of the tradition, history and spirit of Texas A&M. My first visit to the memorial was with an A&M graduate, Freddy Rodriguez. He told me the best time to visit was at night. When we arrived I immediately detected an indescribable atmosphere within the cool evening air. The next aspect that struck me was how silent it was. Even though you could see busy roads in the distance, the noise didn't seem to travel in our direction. The whole experience moved me in a way I hadn't expected. As we slowly walked into the deep shadows of the Stonehenge-like figures, I found myself becoming very emotional. The next day I went back and visited the memorial in sunlight so I could properly read the inscriptions. Before leaving I walked into the middle of The Spirit Ring and noticed people had left pennies on top of a granite circle. It represented the Bonfire stack's center pole, and had the date and time of the collapse: 11-18-1999, 2:42 a.m.

Corps of Cadets: On the same night that Freddy showed me the Bonfire Memorial, he was also keen to further my knowledge on The Corps. As a former cadet himself, he was disappointed to hear that my only experiences of The Corps consisted of seeing people dressed in army gear around campus and witnessing hundreds of skinhead chaps running around the stands at midnight yell. In a bid to further educate me, Freddy gave me a tour of The Quad. This was where the Corps lived. After bumping into someone Freddy knew, we were allowed to check out some living quarters. I was speechless. As I'd viewed some of the nice housing that other students lived in, this was at the other end of the spectrum. Similarly, it took me back to my time at university. During my first year I lived in dorms, but that was five-star luxury compared to The Quad. My compact rectangular dorm had just me in it. These rooms were a similar size, but with three people inhabiting them. This was barely the tip of the iceberg compared to what I was about to be told.

Freshman cadets are not known by their first name. Instead, they are each labeled as "fish." These fishes aren't even privileged enough to live in a room. Therefore, their dorms are known as "holes." Before I asked Freddy to stop making this stuff up, he told me that freshman are not allowed to want, think, like or feel. To compound their misery, they are not permitted to walk on grass or square tiles. I was informed that to get around this, cadets would often lay pieces of paper on grass, and so in the eyes of their superiors they technically can't be punished, because standing on paper isn't a punishable offence. Minutes later, right on cue, we witnessed a fish hopping and weaving between grass and tiles. I couldn't believe what I was seeing.

Yes, I was shocked and struggled to get my head around it all. On the other hand, I was equally fascinated and impressed. I asked myself if I could cope in The Corps. After three seconds, I quickly came to the conclusion that I probably wouldn't last five minutes before the temptation of dancing on grass would prove to be too much. Plus, I like my name. I didn't want to be a fish. Despite this admission, I admired and respected everyone that had a connection to The Corps. It was clear that they played an integral part in preserving the university traditions whilst continuing to represent A&M's prestigious military background.

From the way Freddy glowed as he spoke about his time as a cadet, I could tell the experience helped to positively shape him as a human being. He summed up his time in The Corps as "the most fun I never want to have again."

Silver Taps: In an ideal and perfect world, I wouldn't have experienced this tradition. Silver Taps is held for students who pass away while enrolled at Texas A&M. This tribute takes place on the first Tuesday of the month following a student's passing.

The moment I arrived at the Academic Plaza, I didn't know what to expect. The first thing I noticed was all the lights were out. It was pitch black. Everyone stood perfectly still and in complete silence whilst hymns chimed from the Albritton Tower. At 10:30 p.m. the Ross Volunteer Firing Squad marched through the crowds and fired a twenty-one-gun salute. Following this, buglers played a special rendition of Taps. I didn't know that not a single word would be said throughout. The unique serenity reminded me of my first visit to the Bonfire Memorial. You could really tell this tradition was one that Aggies treasured. Likewise, I was told about stories involving another emotional event called Muster. This takes place every year on April 21st and is a time for Aggies to grieve, reflect and celebrate the lives of people that are no longer with us. Furthermore, it is a gathering that enables you to look to the past, present and future. It is celebrated in over four hundred towns and cities across the world.

19. Road Rage & Fireworks

Deep down, I knew the end of my adventure was creeping closer and closer. In exactly seven days I'd be cramped into an extremely uncomfortable plane seat. Just the thought of it made me recoil. Funnily enough, pondering my next steps in life whilst viewing a generic Tom Cruise sci-fi film and eating rubbery chicken out of a silvery plastic container didn't exactly appeal to me.

Instead of feeling sorry for myself, I was determined to make my last week as memorable as possible. Without warning, it got off to a rousing start. As I walked down South Texas Avenue for the six hundredth time, I noticed a black car shoot out of one of the nearby parking lots. In the process, he very nearly wiped out an oncoming truck.

The truck driver reacted furiously and predictably honked his horn numerous times. So what? I hear you ask. Good question. I was moments away from witnessing some high quality, authentic road rage. Fifty yards down the road, the black car turned into Whataburger to presumably stock up on cheeseburgers and fries. What he probably wasn't expecting was a guest. The truck had sensationally pulled into the American regional fast food restaurant behind him. Cue mayhem in the middle of the parking lot.

"Motherf***er! Where did you learn to drive? You almost f***ed my truck up!"

The surprised expression on the face of the crappy driver was priceless. He was gobsmacked the man in the truck was so infuriated that he had decided to follow him.

"Sorry, sorry. I thought the road was clear. I didn't mean...."

"I don't give a sh**; you shouldn't be allowed on the roads. You're a f***ing kid! Come here!"

By this point the aggressor was spitting expletives into the other man's face. It looked a real possibility that the driver of the black car had just shat himself. Out of nowhere a sentence was muttered that if you'd given me a million guesses of what the petrified individual would say next, I'd probably not have got it.

"Look, to make up for it I'll buy you a burger?"

Silence.

"Fries too? Drink?"

Incredibly, once the irate man had calmed down he agreed to this gesture of goodwill. I was stunned. If trailing someone that cuts you up on the roads leads to getting a free hamburger and fries, I seriously need to start doing it. The whole episode astounded me. Minutes before, the truck driver was threatening to knock this dude out. Now they were on the brink of sitting down and sharing a romantic meal together. The moment I snapped out of my heavily confused status, I thought to myself: *What I'd give to be a fly on the wall for that dinner date...*

What on earth were they going to talk about? Surely it was going to be as wonderfully and excruciatingly awkward as finding an online dating application on your partner's phone.

That's when it hit me: Whataburger is in fact open to anyone. All I needed to do was spend a couple of dollars, sit close to these absorbing protagonists and enjoy the outcome of this remarkable saga. Before you judge me, I'm fully aware that I was effectively stalking these two characters. However, I was intrigued, hungry and more importantly, I literally had nothing better to do.

The outcome was marvelous. Few words were spoken. I had never seen someone wolf down a meal so quickly. Unsurprisingly, the black car driver wanted to leave the burger joint as swiftly as possible. After chomping down his last mouthful, he plucked up the courage to stand to his feet.

"Right, sorry again. I've got to go and pick up…"

"You're not going anywhere," said the truck driver.

"What? Yes I am."

"No. We haven't had dessert yet."

"Huh? I haven't got time. I need to head to Bryan."

"No. You need to go and get us dessert. I'll have a cinnamon roll."

The black car driver looked aghast, but weakly nodded. As he approached the counter you could tell he was caught in two minds. A split second later he'd made his decision. To the amazement of the whole restaurant, he ran full pelt out of the front door and back to his vehicle. The truck driver let out a large sigh and said out loud to himself, "I guess dessert was a long shot."

Every morning I walked the streets of College Station listening to the previous day's exceptional TexAgs Radio podcast.

The dulcet tones of Gabe Bock and friends never failed to supply me with mountains of Aggie football knowledge.

Out of the blue, in my last week I was fortunate enough to be invited into the studio. Andrew and Clay joined me on air to promote their Oscar-worthy production that I'd almost ruined due to having one too many sake bombs. Unsurprisingly, I failed to mention I possessed a rather sketchy radio background. When I was thirteen years old, I used to stay up for hours playing soccer management simulation computer games. Alongside this rather geeky pastime, me and my pals bombarded late-night local radio shows with prank calls. We took it in turns to put on fake accents and see who remained on air the longest. I was victorious under the alias Jean-Pierre. He was a middle-aged French gentleman with a passion for automobiles and baguettes.

The whole team at TexAgs were unbelievably welcoming towards me. I loved everything about the place. During the radio show, Clay reminded me of an anecdote that occurred on the first day we'd met. On my principal visit to TexAgs headquarters, the weather was atrocious. When I turned up it looked like I'd swam there. Once it was time to depart, Andrew asked me if I wanted a lift back to my accommodation. As it had stopped raining, I declined. I wanted to source some lunch on my way back—it proved to be a disastrous judgment call.

Halfway through my mission, the heavens reopened. This time it was ten times worse. It was like several bathtubs of water were being repeatedly poured onto me. Within a few seconds I was completely soaked to the bone. Furthermore, I was worried about my laptop and passport. If the water seeped through my bag I'd be in big trouble. Before I could worry for a second longer, I crossed a road that led to a group of houses. A car behind me pulled into the road and beeped their horn at me. With the amount of hassle I'd received from drivers in the past, I'd assumed they were residents and were pissed off because I'd forced them into braking. I turned around and let loose.

"Are you serious? Look at the f***ing weather!"

"Get in!" It was Clay.

Surreal. Many months before, whilst sat at my desk at work back in England, I had initially discovered TexAgs through one of Clay's productions. It was called "Dragon Slayer" and was a feature on Johnny Manziel's offseason training in San Diego. Now, I was sitting in the front seat of his car and drenching the interior. It's a funny old world.

My final midnight yell practice was an emotional affair. Knowing it would be the last time I'd stand pitch side with Jeff as we watched the 12th Man got to me a little. As the "Spirit of Aggieland" rang out, a small tear rolled down my left cheek. It was the beginning of the end.

President Loftin was being honored; it was his final home game as president. Ironically, I'd bumped into him earlier in the day. On my walk towards the stadium, I saw him standing by the Haynes Ring Plaza. Sensing an opportunity, I marched over and introduced myself. It was a little awkward. I hoped he wouldn't recognize me from our initial encounter at the First Yell concert. Luckily, I got away with it.

It wasn't just the concluding midnight yell for me and President Loftin, it was also the last night that Kyle Field would stand as we knew it. Moments after the Mississippi

State game, the cranes and bulldozers were set to arrive and commence a $450 million renovation project.

As soon as I woke up on the Saturday morning, I couldn't help but notice the poor weather. I had hoped to top up my tan before heading back to cold, wet and dreary England. Alas, maybe a tan wasn't the best idea. Someone with a tan in the UK during the wintery months would stick out like a sore thumb, and I had done more than enough of that in Texas.

On my walk to Kyle Field, I soaked up every last detail. I wanted to remember as much as I possibly could about the gameday experience that I'd fallen head over heels in love with. When I arrived at the tailgate and saw the Barnards, I felt like I was part of their tailgating family. It was home. I was truly flattered when they acknowledged me in the speech before the fabled bucket was handed around.

The day was full of sentiment. I knew that everything I was doing and seeing was for the last time. It was throughout the March of Honor that the occasion got to me the most. The heartbeat of the crowd started to drum as the players ran out. I took the moment in and bottled it up. That feeling of the Aggies taking to the field is like no other. You know it's business time.

In England, they only perform the national anthem before important finals or international tournaments. Yet in the United States, they play the national anthem before every single sporting event. Additionally, in this state they also enact the anthem of Texas. As I had participated in so many American sporting events over the past few months, I'd found myself memorizing pretty much every word of "The Star-Spangled Banner." Sorry, Queen Elizabeth II.

The opponents, Mississippi State Bulldogs, brought back some warm and fuzzy childhood memories. I vividly remembered the dreaded word "Mississippi" regularly popping up in spelling tests at school.

Thanks to a very generous Aggie called Peter Moore, I had one of the best seats in the house for my final pilgrimage to Kyle Field. I was lucky enough to be standing in Section 142, right on the 50-yard line. For once I was a comfortable distance away from the away fans, or so I thought. Halfway into the first quarter, a Bulldogs fan thought it would be a cracking idea to rattle a cowbell directly into my eardrums. To my surprise, it made me slightly nostalgic for home. Portsmouth FC possesses a supporter so fanatical that he went as far as renaming himself by deed poll, John Anthony Portsmouth Football Club Westwood. The man turns up to games with a collection of atrociously out of tune musical instruments. Not only this, but he has almost every inch of his body tattooed with something relating to Pompey. In 2009, I had the double-edged honor of being his next-door neighbor at a hotel in Portugal for a preseason tour. On one particular evening, it was so wild we ended up in a random house party with hundreds of people that could barely speak a word of English. Well, that's not entirely true. There was one bizarre Portuguese gentleman who had learned the language through watching the TV show, *Lost*. I can vaguely remember him shouting the word "Hurley!" every time he downed a pint of lager.

The following morning, me and my friend Rob woke up in the shadows of a small fishing boat. Somehow, we had ended up in the next village along. Furthermore, after checking my phone I noticed I had numerous images of an individual dressed as an ostrich promenading up and down a jetty. To this day I literally have no idea how they got there.

From my delightful midfield position, I had a stellar view of Johnny Manziel's final curtain call at Kyle Field. Despite chants of "one more year" from the student section, it was evident that Johnny was always going to declare for the NFL draft once the season came to a close.

He didn't disappoint, ending the game with a total of 493 offensive yards and five touchdown passes. Other noticeable contributions came from Travis Labhart (102 receiving yards, 2 TD's) and Toney Hurd Jr. who completed one of the most bone crunching sacks I had ever seen. Similarly, Drew Kaser deserved a mention for some sublime punting.

With these displays in the books, Texas A&M held off a late Mississippi State resurgence to hold onto a 51-41 victory. This marked the 700th win of the Aggies football program. To celebrate such a milestone, numerous fireworks were let off. I may have missed Guy Fawkes Night the previous week, but thankfully I'd eventually have my yearly craving of pyrotechnics satisfied.

Overall, it felt like the perfect send off. Yes, there were a couple of blemishes, such as Trey Williams taking a kickoff return back to the house only for it to be chalked off because of a taunting penalty, but in total the occasion yet again delivered. The mixture of an awesome concord-like flyover, a clip of Reveille looking embarrassed as she sat next to the gormless MSU bulldog on the Jumbotron, and finally Johnny jumping into the arms of the 12th Man and singing the Aggie War Hymn put the icing on the cake of a monumentally special adventure.

20. Toppled Tortilla Thrower

Before heading home I still had a night in Houston to negotiate. Oh, and a flight in an aircraft that was probably older than a World War II jet.

It should come as no surprise that I decided against using the hotel in Gunspoint again. Instead, I plumped for accommodation that was situated about twenty feet from George Bush Intercontinental Airport's runway. The place uncontrollably shook every time a plane came in to land. I found it strangely invigorating at first. But following the 300th time, my enthusiasm started to waiver.

That wasn't my only gripe. When I booked my stay, I hadn't realized it was a pet-friendly hotel. You can imagine my surprise when I turned up to check-in at reception. Dogs, cats and even a parrot outnumbered the amount of people surrounding the front desk.

Regardless, I'd been promised my room would be located on the "humans only" floor. They used those exact words. Humans only? What if I fancied venturing onto the aliens floor? I bet they have some high quality parties up there.

I got on with it. In fairness, I wasn't in the best of moods. Obviously, I was sad that I had just left my beloved Aggieland behind. Secondly, another taxi driver had mugged me off. If you're not American, pay attention. Rewind several weeks—I had touched down in Houston after flying in from Pittsburgh. I got into a cab; the driver could obviously gauge that I was from out of town. The very second he dropped me off at my destination, he added a mystical $10 to what the meter read. Without hesitation, I questioned it.

"An extra tenner? How does that work? And why is it not added onto the meter at the start?"

He began to panic because I'd kicked up a fuss. The words "Houston tax" were mumbled in my direction. I looked confused. He finished by explaining that because I was picked up from Terminal C, I had to pay extra. It totaled to $10 more. The incomprehensible part was that the meter said $18.35. Where did he get exactly $10 from? As soon as the car stopped, he quickly worked out what this tax was due to be. He's either a mathematical genius and has gone down the wrong career path, or a blatant charlatan. Like a fool I ended up paying it—I couldn't be bothered to make a scene.

Where am I going with this? Well, the next time I got into a Houston taxi, I put on what I can only describe as a less than authentic Houstonian accent and acted like I was from around town. Yes, you do start to go a little crazy when you've lived in a travel tavern for a number of months. I reached the destination and guess what? I paid exactly what the meter read. There was no Houston or Terminal C tax. Only the price I was meant to pay. Pop, bang, lovely.

On this last day, I completely forgot to play my part as an enthusiastic Texan. I was back to being a bumbling Englishman. Yet again, I was screwed over. A magical, beefed-up price was added to the meter.

A couple of hours later, I had acclimatized to the humans' only floor. Thus far, I was relieved I hadn't seen a cow or mongoose promenading up and down the corridor.

Once the late-afternoon NFL games came to an end, my stomach was rumbling. The memory of the last time I'd gone hunting for food in Houston was fresh in my memory. Fortunately, this time I was prepared. Whilst opening the suspiciously miniscule windows in my hotel room, there she was in all her glory, a green and yellow sandwich shop. I'd never been so happy to see a Subway in all of my life.

I had an extra stride in my step as I walked over to enjoy my pending footlong. I was safe in knowledge that I wouldn't come across any stripper poles, firearms or men with neck tattoos in this establishment. Nope, just wonderful, crisp sandwich goodness.

Every bite that went down was celebrated. By the time I'd finished, I felt like I was on the verge of popping. In hindsight, the extra bag of chips probably wasn't the right call. Irrespective of this, I felt like a king sauntering back to the hotel.

For the rest of the evening I planned to have a quiet one and get some rest before my increasingly daunting flight back home. However, as always, things didn't exactly go to plan. After belly flopping onto the bed, I turned the TV on in the hope I'd be able to watch the build up to NFL Sunday Night Football. Horror struck. A blue screen emblazoned my screen with a message that delivered a feeling that was on par with standing on a plug socket.

"No Signal."

In the wake of frantically pressing every single button on the remote at least seventeen times, I came to the conclusion that an animal such a gazelle or hippopotamus had chewed the satellite receiver to pieces.

The people at reception weren't exactly helpful. I was made aware that they probably weren't the most efficient bunch, as they still had Halloween decorations up eleven days after the occasion had passed.

Not all was lost. On my Subway adventure, I had noticed a bar across the parking lot. My quiet night in was abruptly scrapped. The last thing I wanted to do was sit in front of a TV displaying two upsetting words all evening.

To my relief, this bar was exactly what the doctor ordered. It was quiet, peaceful and had good beers on tap. What more could I ask for? As the Shiner Bock flowed, the place got steadily busier. At first I found this puzzling, as it was a Sunday night. The minute I chatted to a few people at the bar, I soon found out why. This was a regular haunt for the flight attendants to unwind in.

In the background, the Dallas Cowboys were getting their arses handed to them by the New Orleans Saints. A couple of Cowboys fans to my left looked as if they were on the brink of internally combusting.

Once the final whistle was blown, I began to reflect on some bits and pieces. In all honesty, I feared I'd feel lost without College Station, Texas A&M and all the wonderful friends I had made in the last few months. Simply speaking, my life would never be the same. This experience had changed my outlook on everything.

Sensing that I was sinking into a deep train of thought, an airhostess that had been downing shots jumped onto the bar and conducted a dance that almost resulted in her tripping over a selection of glasses and crashing to the floor. Luckily, her heels skillfully evaded an array of beermats, but to the disgust of the bartender, the tip jar was taken as collateral damage.

Her friend wasn't quite so lucky. Moments before, this gentleman had been explaining to me why the people of Texas

Tech are known as "tortilla throwers." He went to university there and didn't take kindly to the news I'd been in town to see their rivals. Shortly after this conversation, I heard a devilish crashing sound. The same character had just fallen off a life-size metal horse that stood elegantly in the corner of the bar. Earlier in the evening he had been pretending to spar like a boxer with the equine. It reminded me of a Newcastle United soccer fan that once punched a police horse in the head, sparking national outrage. Metal Horse 1-0 Texas Tech Alumni.

As he wailed in pain to get attention from the on-looking attractive airhostesses, I enquired if the bartender had a spare tortilla that I could throw at him. No luck. In a sense, it was an ironic ending to my Texan adventure. I hadn't planned a final night out, but behind yet another unturned stone I found a gem.

The next morning I was getting ready to leave the humans only floor when I noticed an anomaly by the elevator. In no uncertain terms, it was a poo. Now don't get me wrong, if you're going to stay in a pet-friendly hotel, it's only natural you're going to observe the odd case of misplaced animal excrement. But I'd been given some assurances. The main one being I'd only be sharing a floor with mankind. I'm not the type of person to question the authorities that run a hotel, even if I did hear a dog barking next door for most of the night. So, I took it at face value. There is no conceivable way an animal could have invaded our floor, right? In that case I could only draw one conclusion. A human had done his or her business by the elevator. A hit and run. The perfect crime.

There was one final port of call before hopping back on a plane to Blighty. All weekend I had been looking forward to revisiting Ruby's Diner—the place that ended my 24-hour hunger the last time I departed Houston. Thankfully, my last meal on American soil didn't disappoint. I would have happily stayed there for eternity.

Instead, I boarded a plane that was so old I was worried it might not actually get off the ground. My initial fears were reinforced when we were delayed at the terminal for two hours due to an issue with the hydraulics. Technical language like hat doesn't exactly fill a nervous flyer with much confidence. Nonetheless, I had my own problems to deal with. Once I'd located my spot in row F, I naturally leaned back to find a comfortable position. To my surprise, the back of the seat fully reclined. Had I struck gold and been upgraded to business class without knowing? Why else had I been given a bed? I hadn't. Eventually, it dawned on me that my headrest was now effectively hovering on top of the lap of the unfortunate middle-aged man seated directly behind me. The seat was broken in two.

After embarrassingly apologizing countless times, I pressed the button that summons a flight attendant. Within seconds, one swooped in, turned my button off and strode away.

"Erm, excuse me! My seat is cut in half."

That promptly got their attention. I was moved to the other side of the plane and got to enjoy the benefits of a fully functional chair. I planned to sit back, watch some movies, and look forward to knocking back some grade A fish and chips once we landed.

Unfortunately, the movies part didn't go to plan. You know you're in trouble when *Grown Ups 2* is on the front cover of the entertainment magazine.

21. No Longer Marooned

Gloomy, grim, depressing, dismal and cheerless. No, I am not describing the food that was served on the plane. Instead, it's a group of adjectives that most accurately describe the English climate in mid-November.

When I stepped off the ageing Boeing 747, it dawned on me that I'd made a terrible error. I was still wearing the clothes I'd strolled down South Texas Avenue in. Wearing such gear can only end in one result—hypothermia. It was like arriving on another planet. Everyone was pacing around in multiple layers. And yet there I was, with my shorts and knobbly knees on display.

Fog swirled around London Heathrow Airport like a menacing and chilling demon. The subzero temperatures heightened my tired and faltering senses. I was back. Home sweet home.

The first few days on British soil were peculiar. Once my body clock readjusted, I came to terms with no longer eating red meat or drinking Shiner Bock on a daily basis. Furthermore, I had no job or idea what my next chapter in life would entail. All I really knew was that Texas A&M still had two road games on their schedule. Additionally, with a current 8-2 record, a reputable Bowl game was possibly in the pipeline.

To make that goal a reality, they had to roll into Baton Rouge and slay a highly regarded SEC rival in the form of Louisiana State University. As with the Arkansas and Ole Miss games, I felt guilty for not being there. The moment pictures filtered through of an Aggie invasion of Bourbon Street, I was left frustrated that instant transportation technology had not yet been developed. Come on scientists, pull your fingers out.

My apartment is positioned a stone's throw from Guildford High Street. Subsequently, I decided to bring a slice of Bourbon Street to my sleepy, Surrey town. To the sheer disgust of Katie, I hung an array of Aggie flags out of the windows and around the apartment.

Once the game kicked off, I wondered what my neighbors made of me shouting the building down with cries of, "F***ing get him!" "Get open!" and "Come on, Johnny!"

In the days and weeks that followed, it came as no surprise when I received bemused and questionable looks every time I shared an elevator with the people that were within earshot.

Whilst LSU's running back, Kenny Hilliard, ran in for LSU's fourth touchdown of the afternoon, I was on the brink of throwing the coffee table out of the window. Fortunately for the people on the street below, I refrained from doing so.

Texas A&M fell to a punishing 34-10 defeat. To further add salt to the wound, during halftime CBS played a *Mike & Molly* commercial over the Fightin' Texas Aggie Band's performance. I was literally suicidal.

The following week whizzed by. The hours spent eating generic salt-flavored crisps and watching documentaries about three-legged mammoths all merged into one.

In between this plethora of excitement, it can sometimes be a struggle to keep up with reality. The realization I had £3.46 left to my name was starting to hit home.

At the midweek point I left my apartment for the first time in three days. Yes, three days. The sunlight kicked me square in the kneecaps. I felt like retreating back to my cave. Luckily, a group of black clouds negotiated the situation with admirable charisma.

To be honest, I wasn't looking my best. After plucking up the courage to re-enter a world where my remote control isn't king, I hadn't bothered to think about much else.

As I approached the local supermarket and weaved through Christmas shoppers like a heavy, third-down running back, someone came towards me. I hadn't bargained for any human interaction. After all, I'd just nipped out to restock on necessities, such as chicken, cereal and beer. Yet here I was, being shouted at from across the road. Who were they? What did they want?

"Are you looking for part time or full time work, sir?"

Really? Was it that obvious? I looked at my reflection in a nearby shop window. I was wearing a shabby coat, ragged woolly hat and some withered sweatpants that I only ever bring out of the closet when I'm hungover. Likewise, I was unshaven and probably yawning.

Fair play, I thought. Let's see what career path they had in mind. Maybe they could send me back to the Lone Star State? Before I even had an opportunity to assess the line of scrimmage, the next three words hit me in the face like a super truck.

"Trash Can Management."

First off, I hadn't even heard or seen these words put together before.

"You'd be emptying trash cans in the local area."

Thanks for the clarification.

Now don't get me wrong, I have nothing against people in the trash can management industry. I'm sure it has its perks and a fair amount of glamour, but it wasn't for me.

I sloped back to my apartment asking myself the same question. Why did they go straight in with that particular profession? Why not start a bit higher and work their way down?

As I re-entered my flat, I saw myself properly in the mirror. Oh yeah, that's why. I looked like a zombie. Moments later I showered, shaved and burned the clothes I'd worn. I then consoled myself with cereal and beer.

Days later, Thanksgiving rolled around. I'm not going to lie; I am a little jealous that I have never experienced a traditional American Thanksgiving before. In the UK, nothing like it exists. Probably because we don't have a great deal to be thankful for. Well, I guess that's not strictly true. I consider the fact that our local fish and chips shop hasn't shut down yet to be a massive bonus.

Unfortunately, my Thursday did not consist of getting the family together, eating as much as we humanly could, and watching three back-to-back football games. I had a far more elaborate plan up my sleeve—tucking into a £1 turkey sandwich from the nearby convenience store. It didn't end there. Oh no, all the trimmings surrounded me. I'm fairly sure I had enough sausages, scotch eggs and chicken drumsticks to last me a lifetime.

People often wonder what heaven is like, but I'm sure my setup was pretty close to the mark, even if the turkey in my sandwich probably wasn't turkey. For £1, I'm guessing it might have been anything disguised as turkey. The mind boggles. I'm probably safer not knowing. On second thought, I was probably safer not eating it. Regardless, it slipped down seamlessly as the memories from the first Thanksgiving after my family moved to America came flooding back. At the time I was distraught. Now, I look back and view it as a major turning point in my life. Without the realization that I'd sunk into a quagmire of discontent, I'd almost certainly still be residing in the same dreary square mile and continuing my sterling role as an unappreciated and lifeless desk monkey.

Thankfully, I survived the alarmingly cheap sandwich and was gearing up for Texas A&M's final regular season game. With a 12:45 a.m. kickoff in the UK, it resulted in the unique challenge of trying to stay awake for all four quarters. Luckily, over the last couple of years, I had devised a strategy that is purely designed to see me through until the immoral hours of the morning. One factor is always key—preparation. Take Super Bowl XLVII for example. If I hadn't prepared in the right way, the dreaded power outage would have definitely claimed me as a casualty. Instead, I held on with my pride intact.

Firstly, pace yourself. Don't blow your load. I know how tempting and glorious those beers look from 9:00 a.m. onwards. However, any foolish moves will leave you swimming in a large pool of regret. Quite simply, any alcohol consumed early doors will result in you failing to go the distance. Unsurprisingly, this is often the weakest chink in my armor.

Similarly with food, it is imperative you do not keep stuffing your face throughout the day. Relax. Let the chips, wings and microwave pizzas mature like a fine wine. You will know deep down when you're ready to indulge.

The next aspect to consider is the role played by your number one ally—the fridge. Regular visits to this white wildebeest will help the circulation in your body. Moreover, you are open to take a detour once in a while to offload the heavy amounts of beer and/or grub that you've thrown down your neck.

Beer is a subject in itself. What do you go for? The possibilities are endless. This is the final SEC clash of the season. It demands the very best. Whilst standing in the supermarket, I was torn between a nice, upmarket European option and Sam Adams. Sod it, if in doubt—get both. After all, I'd earned it after glugging down the cheap and nasty stuff the week before.

The final facet to consider is your surroundings. The above should only ever take place in an indoor facility that's affectionately known as a Man Cave. This location should represent everything that's right in the world. As well as being a multimedia heaven (a minimum of two screens is advised), it must also be a shrine to kooky football merchandise and memorabilia.

Again, the flags were erected around the apartment. In the hours leading up to the game against Missouri, I was already doing the "Carlton Dance" from *The Fresh Prince of Bel-Air*. Coach Sumlin had announced he was staying in Aggieland, and had signed a six-year contract extension. The man, the legend, the badass, was staying.

That wasn't the only positive. Auburn had just beaten Alabama in one of the most dramatic finishes to a college football game in the history of the sport. With one second remaining on the clock, the scores were tied. With the last play of the contest, Alabama had an ambitious field goal attempt from 57 yards. As the ball approached the posts, it died in the air. Auburn's Chris Davis caught it and ran it back to the house for a touchdown. Cue pandemonium in the stands. Alabama's dreams of a National Championship hat-trick were in tatters.

Their suffering didn't end there either. A few weeks later, they had their butts slapped by the Oklahoma Sooners in the Sugar Bowl. Even from 5,000 miles away, I couldn't help but smirk and think of those tiresome bammers who taunted me on September 14th. Who was laughing now?

In terms of the bigger picture, it was yet another justification of my trip. Those moments summed up exactly why I wanted to experience a season of the behemoth that is college football. Each campaign is comparable to a zombie movie with every team desperate to outlast and not slip up. There really is no sport that even comes close—every week is a season. One loss and your National Championship dreams are over.

Within the mountains of chips and pizza, I was also making a real effort to be healthy. And by healthy, I mean having a slice of lime with my beer. What? It counts as one of your five fruit and vegetables a day, right?

My hunger wasn't being helped by the fact the colors of Missouri distinctively reminded me of Buffalo Wild Wings. I longed for their legendary cheeseburger slammers.

Another thing I couldn't fail to notice was that I was being haunted by Beckhams: Odell Beckham at LSU the week before, Dorial Green-Beckham at Missouri and David Beckham in England.

Before I dwelled on this unremarkable coincidence any longer, the game kicked off. At halftime the Aggies were somehow holding onto a 14-7 lead. Unfortunately, it didn't take long for Mizzou to fight back and force a switch of the most important aspect of football—momentum. In the last few months, I had heard the "M" word shouted from rooftops every time I'd watched a game. In many ways, it's reminiscent of when you play golf. You can be racking up countless triple bogeys and then out of nowhere you hit a couple of beauties, and suddenly your talents wouldn't look out of place on the PGA Tour. Football had an uncanny knack of going down a similar path. One defining moment often turned a matchup completely on its head.

It was 3:30 a.m. I heard a group of pie-eyed strangers shouting in the street. My presumption was they were celebrating Ben Malena's touchdown that had just tied the game at 21-21. Their joyous sounds quickly turned sour as Mizzou's Henry Josey ran in for a 57-yard touchdown. The game finished 28-21. At 4:08 a.m. I slumped to bed hoping I'd wake up to the news I'd dreamt the second half and that the Aggies held on to secure a victory. Regrettably, this did not happen.

With an 8-4 record in the books, Texas A&M was penciled into the Chick-fil-A Bowl. Their opponents? The Duke Blue Devils.

I felt a sense of irony that A&M ended up in this particular Bowl game. Every day, I walked past a Chick-fil-A on South Texas Avenue whilst pacing around College Station. The fumes that filtered out often seemed irresistible.

Curiously, the game was scheduled to take place on the evening of December 31st. With a five-hour time difference, the game kicked off at 1:00 a.m. on January 1st 2014 in England.

As is custom on New Year's Eve, I proceeded to get on the alcoholic sauce as early as lunchtime. My usual cautious preparation had gone out of the window. The occasion saw us have some friends over for an evening of fun festivities; even the Aggie War Hymn got an outing. With every bottle of Corona that went through my system, I knew making it through until four or five in the morning was going to take some sort of miracle.

Eventually, after seeing London's Big Ben chime us into the New Year, I was only an hour away from seeing my beloved Aggies take to the field in Atlanta.

The first half couldn't have gone any worse. On both sides of the ball, A&M was in tatters. Their ACC rivals were leading 38-17 at halftime. Despite this precarious position, I firmly held onto the belief that Johnny Manziel would turn the game on its head. In the second half I retreated to the bedroom to watch the rest on my iPad while dipping in and out of consciousness.

Luckily, I was just about awake for Johnny's unforgettable scramble that took place early in the third quarter. It was reminiscent of the truly remarkable play against Alabama in 2012 when he pulled a rabbit of a hat and found Ryan Swope at the back of the end zone. On this occasion, with the play seemingly broken down and Johnny heading to the floor, he bounced through a wedge of offensive lineman and found a wide-open Travis Labhart who ran the ball in for a touchdown. Needless to say, it forced that trusty thing called momentum.

Following scenes of such nature, in his final game wearing the maroon and white, Johnny Manziel delivered a rallying cry to his troops. Following every play he was a man possessed. There was no way he was going to accept defeat, and 455 offensive yards later, he wasn't to be denied. Texas A&M completed an epic comeback to win the Chick-fil-A Bowl, 52-48.

The Aggies finished 18th in the College Football 2013 Associated Press poll. Although there were whispers at the start of the campaign about a National Championship being hoisted around the East Texas region, A&M couldn't feel too hard done by. Consequently their inexperienced and erratic defense that forced Aggies all around the world to hide behind couches, caught up with them.

However, following decades of failing to reach their potential, the tides are now steadily turning. With Kevin Sumlin at the helm, Ags everywhere should never dare to dream. In addition, the perception of A&M living in the shadow of the Longhorns is certainly over. In the end the so-called "superpower" University of Texas failed to rank in the top 25. Just like the bammers, who's laughing now?

22. Open Letter

Following the season opener against Rice, a mother from Johnny Manziel's hometown, Kerrville, sent him an open letter that urged him to become a better role model to her sixth-grade son. I have decided to carry the torch and pen an open letter myself.

Dear Various,

Firstly, how can I not kick things off with a golden shout out to the 12th Man? You were a constant heartbeat throughout my stay in Aggieland—I am proud and humbled to claim that I got to stand amongst you, at ready.

Next up, the man at the helm, Coach Kevin Sumlin.

You possess so much swag that it's almost blatantly unfair to the other college football coaches up and down the country. Every time you speak, I am fixed into a bottomless trance that would unquestionably see me run through a brick wall at your request.

In my final days in Aggieland, someone asked me about my biggest regret of the adventure. There was only one answer. It was not getting to meet the man behind the badass sunglasses.

The pressure must be extraordinary. Each week you have 90,000 wannabe coaches shouting advice at you. I often wondered what was going through your mind as you walked back to the dressing room at halftime. You'd be bombarded with people shouting generic bile such as, "CHANGE THE DEFENSE!" Without a flinch, you marched with honor and dignity.

Under your guidance, A&M has come on leaps and bounds. That viewpoint is small change to some, but at the beginning of 2012 analysts were claiming the Aggies would be perennial underdogs and do well to win a single game in the SEC. Now, A&M are serious contenders in every matchup.

Some sections will be quick to point out that players such as Manziel, Evans and Matthews are leaving for the NFL. Yes, maybe. However, A&M isn't an isolated incident. Every college has similar issues. Others need to realize that those stars were not the high point in A&M's footballing history, they were the catalyst. Who do I want at the helm to make sure such a catalyst transcends A&M into one of the hottest and most successful football programs in the country? Who do I trust? Easy! It's Kevin 'damn' Sumlin.

Next up—Johnny, Johnny, Johnny.

I am not a mother. I do not have a sixth-grade son (that I know of). I am not from your hometown. Instead, I am a bumbling Englishman that clocked up over 20,000 miles in 2013 to watch you play at Kyle Field each week.

A few years ago, I didn't even like what us Brits call, "American Football." I always thought there were far too many commercials, it was too stop-start, and the fact games kicked off at 1.30 a.m. GMT was a massive pain in the bottom.

My folks eventually moved to Pittsburgh. When I visited them, people only talked about one thing: football. Naturally,

I got into it. Watching the Steelers was great fun, but something always felt like it was missing. There was never one player that made me sit in awe or jump out of my seat with excitement, until I first saw you perform. Quite simply, you were a major factor behind me falling in love with the sport. Everything about watching you play, the stadium, the fans, the atmosphere, you scrambling, made me want to sample it first hand. I needed a piece of that pie.

After spending a majority of the 2013 football season in College Station, it's surreal to consider if I hadn't watched that first game against Florida, or discovered your abilities, I would never have experienced one of the most special places I've ever been to.

You've done yourself and Texas A&M justice. Every Aggie can say they were extremely lucky to witness what you've achieved. Likewise, I've never seen a society root for someone in such a passionate way. On countless occasions I observed Aggies in bars all over the Brazos Valley celebrate incomplete passes from Heisman rivals as if they'd won the lottery.

You are rare. Very rare. You're one sportsman that when you play, every single person in the room will stop what they are doing just to watch what crazy stunt you will pull next. There really is nothing like it.

It makes me genuinely sad that we will never see you pull on the maroon and white again. Thank you.

PS. During my most recent birthday, the second I blew the candles out on my cake I wished for you to be drafted with the first overall pick by the Houston Texans. As you ended up going to the Steelers divisional rivals, Cleveland Browns. I'm officially never having a birthday again.

Right, it's time to cheer myself up. Mike Evans—a day doesn't go by when I don't raise a smile thinking about you running the length of Kyle Field to punch in a touchdown against Alabama. That was truly special and a memory I'll never forget. Throughout the NFL draft, I selfishly had my fingers crossed that you'd fall to the Steelers with the fifteenth pick. Unfortunately, it wasn't to be. Regardless, I will track your career with a keen eye, and hopefully get to watch you run for a 95-yard touchdown in the flesh again one day.

Jake Matthews, there's no way to describe you other than Mr. Solid. I'm no offensive line expert, but even I appreciated how you'd literally erect a wall on Johnny's blindside. I personally dislike when people cascade pressure onto me, however I'd be amazed if you're not a constant Pro Bowler throughout your career. It was a pleasure to see you putting on a clinic of how to play left tackle each week. Moreover, similarly with Johnny and Mike, I found myself getting emotional on the day you were drafted in the first round of the 2014 NFL draft.

Travis Labhart—You were easily the player I related to the most. Every week you wore your heart on your sleeve. For me, you went under the radar in terms of just how good you were. During Johnny's scrambling, he could always be safe in the knowledge that you'd somehow find separation and get open. That remarkable touchdown in the Chick-fil-A Bowl was the perfect example. I was delighted to hear you won the Aggie Heart Award. Perhaps from now on, it can be known as the LabHeart Award?

Every single other player also deserves a mention. From Trey "Twinkle Toes" Williams all the way to punter, Drew "The Laser" Kaser, I was honored to see every one of you pull on the maroon and white.

The most important mention and biggest thanks goes to everyone in Aggieland who made my stay as special as it was.

My first almighty thank you goes to Jeff and Tommy, who from my very first day in Aggieland treated me like family. From Jeff giving me the keys to his place for the Alabama weekend to Tommy taking me to a Houston Texans game, I was constantly overwhelmed by their hospitality. They will forever be like big brothers to me.

Next is my main man, Zach. We spent many evenings in Sully's kibitzing about a wide range of stuff. When I came back to England, it depressed me that I no longer had him to turn to. He's the sort of friend who's worth his weight in gold. On my last day I gave him a Portsmouth FC shirt and apologized for forcing him to support my insignificant soccer team. In return, he gave me a huge "SAW 'EM OFF" flag. It now hangs proudly. Whenever I see it, I always wonder how he and his almighty German Shepherd, Ranger, are getting on. In the future, it's my mission to get him to hop over the pond and live through the wonders of Fratton Park.

Clay and Andrew were a huge part of my adventure. As well as integrating me into the TexAgs environment, they were beacons of light throughout. I knew if I ever needed any help they were just a text or phone call away. Their "An Englishman's Guide to Aggie Football" production displayed their marvelous talents, and helped to put me on the map. Again, I will always regard them as pals for life. I hope they are regularly checking to see if Marge the hoarder is OK.

My tailgating family always elevated my gameday experience. A huge thank you to the Barnards, Andy, JD, Derek and everyone else that was a part of the "Keep the Spirit" tailgate. Going to soccer games now pales in comparison. Each week I try and drum up the enthusiasm to spark the tailgating trend.

I haven't had any luck so far. It's going to be odd imagining them at their tent in future seasons before games. I will sorely miss it.

Some notable mentions also go to Mark, the owner of Sully's Sports Grill & Bar, as well as all the staff that worked there. I hope he's still piling through episodes of *Top Gear* at a rapid rate and all his girls are prospering.

Also, Freddy, who introduced me to many of the great Aggie traditions, deserves a big pat on the back. Moreover, Mark and Brittney made my New York Aggies experience what it was. I loved catching up with them back in Aggieland.

A penultimate shout out goes to TexAgs and Good Bull Hunting. Both were instrumental in giving me a platform to work on. I am eternally grateful to both for their help with everything.

Finally, my family and friends back home. I know it's a terrible cliché and that's why I'll keep it brief, but without their love and support, none of the last few hundred pages would have been possible. For that, I can never thank them enough. Oh, and Mum and Dad, if in the unlikely event you ever fancy a family holiday to Texas, I will love you even more.

23. So Long, Aggieland

When my idea of traveling across the Atlantic and experiencing college football was originally born, I wanted to grasp a wide range of different colleges and stadiums.

Similarly, as soon as I came up with the initial concept, I wanted to further educate people that struggled to understand the whirlwind and hysteria surrounding college football. Throughout my voyage I often thought back to those characters in my local pub that turned their noses up at the sport. Naturally, in every culture people dismiss what they do not understand.

Will Brits ever recognize and appreciate college football? Who knows? In reality, the more exposure it gets, the stronger its presence will become. Hopefully my musings have gone some way to helping that transition. Only time will tell.

In the end, due to the fact I had not won the lottery, visiting numerous colleges was not logistically possible. Instead, I decided to choose one location. In hindsight, I'm over the moon that I went down this path. Aggieland proved to be more than I could have ever wished for.

On the morning of 10th November, I felt like I'd been convicted of a crime and was now waiting to be transported to the nearest jail. In reality, I was waiting for the Ground Shuttle to come and pick me up. I willed my phone not to ring—the last thing I wanted to do was return to England.

The night before my departure, I hadn't slept much. I sat on the edge of my bed and looked out onto a section of nearby road. Whilst street signs swayed in the wind, torrential rain cannoned down.

Before I knew it, the rain dispersed and the sun started to rise. Many months ago I woke up in Aggieland for the first time.

Now, I could hear the vibrations from my phone on the bedside table. All of my belongings were jammed into a suitcase that sat patiently in the corner of the empty and soulless room. It was time to leave College Station.

Lugging my stuff down the staircase proved to be difficult. The excessive purchases from Aggieland Outfitters were clearly having an adverse effect. Comically, the driver looked unconcerned as I nearly toppled head first into the concrete below.

Our bus had various people to pick up around the area. I wasn't fussed; I would have happily driven around the town for hours. On second thought, I'd probably have raised a smile if the bus had broken down. It might have been an omen that I should stay.

Alas, there was no fault. Passenger after passenger hoisted themselves into the back of our Houston-bound vehicle. With this, I received one last beautiful lap of South Texas Avenue. In addition, we got to go past the campus, Northgate and even the outskirts of Bryan for one final time. I fondly remembered reading disparaging comments about Bryan all those months ago. Such concerns were put to bed every time I visited there; I always came away stuffed to the core with copious amounts of succulent, fulfilling food. On the topic of food—oddly, seeing Denny's brought about a tinge of emotion. I realized this was perhaps the first and only time that someone had felt sentimental towards a Denny's before. It reminded me of my very first morning in Aggieland when I sat in a booth, ate a Lumberjack Slam and wondered what the immediate future would bring.

Ultimately, the time eventually came to roll out of C-Stat. I thought back to my concluding train journey home from work in August. Back then I had lingering doubts about my pending adventure. As the train trundled towards each station, I felt dejected and sorrowful, because I had no idea if what I was doing made any sense.

Now, as I watched Kyle Field getting smaller and smaller in the distance, my emotions were at the opposite end of the spectrum. I'd done it.

As sad and heartbreaking as it was to leave Aggieland, my mood was dominated with a feeling of triumph. I came away with a defining experience that will stay with me for the rest of my life.

My reaction to heading back to the UK was mixed. Whilst I was looking forward to seeing friends and family, it was English society that I knew I would feel most frustrated with. In Texas, I had become accustomed to walking anywhere in public and people giving me the time of day. Back in England, if you said hello or smiled at a stranger they'd think you're either an oddball or making a sexual advance—or both. Furthermore, once on George Bush Drive a Mormon said howdy to me. I can safely say a Mormon sighting in the UK would be as rare as sharing a cup of tea with the Lochness Monster.

A particular quote I'd heard dozens of times during my stay in Aggieland will always remain with me. "From the outside looking in, you can't understand it. And from the inside looking out, you can't explain it."

There are no words that portray Texas A&M any better. When I describe the place to outsiders, they struggle to comprehend what I'm saying. In mid-December, I was watching NFL Sunday Night Football with a friend that had little interest in the sport. The Pittsburgh Steelers were playing the Cincinnati Bengals, and as the TV network individually introduced the Steelers offense, the Steelers center took stage.

"Cody Wallace, Texas A&M."

I immediately let out the loudest "WHOOP!" of my life. My friend was stunned.

"Corr blimey! That place really got under your skin?"

Yes, yes it had.

What strikes me the most about the current students and alumni is that everyone is tremendously honored to be a part of this special university. It is an integral chunk of their lives. Whether it is wearing the Aggie ring with deep gratification or signing their class after their name, everything about the place is infectious.

When I compare it to how I feel about the university I attended, it hits home. I have zero connection to my former place of study. Strictly speaking, it was a means to an end. Texas A&M is different. You are made to feel like part of a family. In some way, I now felt accepted into this family.

Yes, I may well be a bandwagon or t-shirt fan on paper. However, I never arrived with the sole intention of becoming an Aggie. I came as a writer. After you've experienced College Station's unique atmosphere, made lifelong friends and stood with the 12th Man at Kyle Field, it's increasingly difficult to remain impartial. I'd go as far as saying 99% of people's blood turns maroon when they sample the history, traditions and spirit of A&M.

Once you grasp the understanding of Aggieland, you can't shake it. I may never have the honor of wearing an Aggie ring, but that doesn't take away what College Station has given me. Deep down, I firmly believe that Texas A&M transformed me into a better person. Just before attending my final midnight yell practice, I was striding to Kyle Field. As I approached the Big Aggie Ring that stands outside the Haynes Ring Plaza, I noticed a family of three taking pictures in front of it. Previously, I would have kept my head down and walked on. On this occasion, I stopped and asked if they wanted me to take a picture of all three of them together with the big ring in the background. They gleefully said yes. Granted, it's not like I did something heroic like saving an infant from a burning building, but I would never have dreamed of going that extra mile before.

As stated, I may not be an Aggie in the conventional sense, but I now proudly possess a maroon heart. Moreover, from this day forward, I wouldn't contemplate having my picture taken without a cheeky thumb on display.

The Brazos Valley can be 5,000 or 10,000 miles away, but to me it does not matter. From here on, whatever I do or wherever I go, I know that I'll always be carrying a piece of Aggieland around with me. It will forever be my second home.

When the bus finally exited the perimeters of College Station and Kyle Field was reduced to a mere dot on the horizon, the adventure was slammed shut. Regardless, I didn't leave thinking it was goodbye. I left feeling… I'll be back.

Overtime

When the train leisurely crawled into Highbury & Islington station, I felt a spate of butterflies encapsulate the pit of my beer belly.

In the merry depths of April, I was enjoying a splendid Saturday afternoon. Before I had time to fully appreciate the balmy spring atmosphere, I found myself in a charming, tasteful and cost-effective supermarket.

I assessed each aisle like a bird of prey. As well as noticing that quarter pounder beef burgers were suspiciously listed at half-price, an imposing banner claimed that watermelons were under the jurisdiction of buy one, get one free. Needless to say, I punched the air with joy.

On my travels to the nearby park, to the general surprise of an on-looking mob at a bus stop, I threw one of the watermelons I'd acquired at a lamppost. In the midst of the gasps, screams and other appreciative noises, I basked in my achievement. The watermelon was now edible. Likewise, the park was in my sights.

During a measured approach, my jaw laboriously ached as I attempted to get my chops around the melon-y goodness. Fortunately, my concentration was soon interrupted. There she was in the distance, in all her dignified glory.

A maroon Texas A&M flag.

Accompanied by a well-constructed gazebo, this flag fluctuated in the unpredictable wind. I was in awe.

Whilst countless people shouted, "Howdy!" in my general direction, I filled up with an immense sense of pride as I congregated with the London Texas A&M club to celebrate Aggie Muster.

Despite the weather zigzagging from lovely sunshine to torrential rain throughout the day, nothing was going to break the famous and legendary Aggie spirit—not even a lousy park ranger who informed us we had to dismantle the gazebo because we didn't hold a permit. *Hiss.*

Even though I had never met any of these Aggies before, it did not matter. To me, they did not feel like strangers. Instead, when y'all wearing maroon and you throw in a case of beer and some half-price meat on the grill, everyone is family.